Facing Death:
Images, Insights,
and Interventions

Facing Death: Images, Insights, and Interventions

A Handbook for Educators, Healthcare Professionals, and Counselors

Sandra L. Bertman, Ph.D.
University of Massachusetts Medical Center
Worcester, Massachusetts

Taylor & Francis
Publishers since 1798

FACING DEATH: IMAGES, INSIGHTS, AND INTERVENTIONS
A Handbook for Educators, Healthcare Professionals, and Counselors

 4 5 6 7 8 9 0   B R B R   9 8 7 6 5 4

This book was set in Collage by Hemisphere Publishing Corporation. The editors were Patricia Dewey and S. Michele Nix; the designer was Debra Eubanks Riffe; the production supervisor was Peggy M. Rote; and the typesetter was Darrell D. Larsen, Jr. Cover design by Debra Eubanks Riffe.
Printing and binding by Braun-Brumfield, Inc..

A CIP catalog record for this book is available from the British Library.

∞ Printed on acid-free paper.

Library of Congress Cataloging-in-Publication Data

Bertman, Sandra L.
    Facing death : images, insights, and interventions : a handbook
for educators, healthcare professionals, and counselors / Sandra L.
Bertman.
        p.   cm. — (Series in death education, aging, and health care)
    Includes bibliographical references and index.
    1. Thanatology.   2. Death—Psychological aspects.   3. Death in
literature.   4. Death in art.   I. Title.   II. Series
HQ1073.5.U6B47   1991
306.9—dc20
                                                                          91-12222
                                                                          CIP
ISBN 0-89116-891-5 (case)
ISBN 1-56032-223-3 (paper)
ISSN 0275-3510

Death ends a life but not a relationship . . .

In loving memory

Freda and Max Borkum
Bess and Edward Bertman
Louise Zelermyer

Contents

Foreword   ix
Preface   xi

Chapter 1   Establishing the Perspective   1

*Terminal illness in contemporary society and the use of the arts to
stimulate dialogue, reveal concerns, enable grieving, and provide consolation*

    Terminal Illness   5
    Interacting with the Arts: Why and How   5
    Notes   8
    References   9

Chapter 2   Images: Facing Death   11

*The introduction of critical themes through a selection of images from the
arts, literature, and popular culture*

    Theme I: The Art of Dying: The Chosen Death   15
    Theme II: Death and Afterlife: Views of Mortality
        and Immortality   23
    Theme III: Far Worse than the Tumor: Existential
        Aloneness   39
    Theme IV: Autonomy, Loss of Control, Unmentionable
        Feelings, Grief   55
    Theme V: Tolerance for Ambivalence: The Land of the Sick
        versus the Land of the Well   67
    Theme VI: The Moment of Death   77
    Epilogue: The Birds of Sorrow: A Coexistence   87
    Notes   98
    References   98

Chapter 3   Responses to the Images   101

*Methodology, utilization of, and responses to the images in five group
settings*

    Responses of Junior and Senior High School Students
        (Science Award Finalists), West Virginia   103

Responses of Graduate Students, Lesley College,
  Cambridge, MA   107
Responses of Medical Students, University of Massachusetts
  Medical School, Worcester, MA   120
Responses of Graduate Nurses, University of Massachusetts
  School of Nursing, Boston, MA   145
Most Memorable Image   150
Responses of Hospice Volunteers, State-Wide Conference,
  Massachusetts   152
Discussion   158
Notes   163

Chapter 4 Broadening the Perspective   165

Facing Death: Guidelines for Using the Arts   169
Facing Death: Some Counseling Guidelines   197

Bibliography and Additional Reading   203

Appendix 1 Death Attitude Questionnaire   209

Appendix 2 Facing Death: A Most Memorable Image   211

Appendix 3 Medical School: First-Year Course Syllabus   213

Foreword

Death is no longer a skeleton in the closet due to the efforts of the modern thanatological movement these past three decades. We are now heir to an informing knowledge base emerging from clinical discernments and empirical findings. Contributions to this base, however, have been fueled essentially by the biological and behavioral sciences. Influence of the arts and humanities has tended to be peripheral. Dr. Bertman realized this impoverishment and void about two decades ago. Since then, in various national and international fora, she has instructed and sensitized the thanatological community to the pertinence and richness of materials available through visual and literary images. The result has been a boon for patient, death educator, and clinician.

This book represents an advancing systematic exposition of her thinking and endeavors in the field. With astuteness and resourcefulness, she has underscored how the arts can provide not only a vital adjunct in teaching and counseling for the thanatologist but also serve as an avenue for self-discovery. She is furnishing us with an educational and therapeutic took of tremendous evocative power for the death educator and counselor in forwarding catharsis and self-knowledge. Findings issuing from the various populations she describes in the book also suggest possibilities for developing a more relevant orientation toward contemporary death and grief.

Dr. Bertman is a superb teacher whose book is germane not only for the death educator and counselor but for all health-care givers in deepening their perceptions of the human condition and personal destiny. Its contribution is summed-up in her own poetic statement—the arts cannot stay the flights of the birds of sorrow but they can help us to better appreciate and endure them.

Herman Feifel, Ph.D.
Psychology Service
U.S. Department of Veterans Affairs
Los Angeles, CA

Preface

This book grew primarily out of my work during the past 15 years as a faculty member at the University of Massachusetts Medical Center, where I created the program in Medical Humanities. Through this program I have taught medical students; have trained counselors, nurses, and house staff; and have offered seminars periodically for patients and family members through the Division of Oncology. In the outpatient clinic these somewhat impromptu meetings, entitled "Far Worse than the Tumor" or "Living with Cancer" (and now in other settings "Living with AIDS"), were offered to patients and whomever accompanied them for chemotherapy and other treatments. These one-shot sessions led to further meetings with individual families and with patient support groups (cancer, AIDS, bereavement). They also have been expanded into ongoing offerings for the medical center at large: "To Know of Suffering," "Who Owns One's Life?," and "The Language of Grief and the Art of Consolation."

The bulk of this experience has emerged as a set of arena-style, double-slide presentations (two slides projected simultaneously on two screens) of literary, artistic, and pop-culture images, which are adapted to suit these various audiences, both at the University of Massachusetts Medical Center and at universities, hospitals, and hospices across the country. More recently, my presentations have assumed a "training" role for individuals involved in teaching and counseling supervision. Accordingly, insofar as is possible, I have attempted to "translate" my slide presentations into handbook form in an attempt to assist professionals whose main concern is to support persons facing terminal illness.

The aim of this text is to support frontline staff who continue to "be there" despite nearly impossible demands and frequent painful losses in this most difficult yet rewarding line of work. Like any good curriculum, this program is in a constant state of growth and evolution; adjustments are continually being made based on what students, counselors, healthcare professionals, patients, and their loved ones teach me. This book should not be viewed as an immutable or static document. Its goal is to be adaptable to the individual's personal teaching or counseling style. I hope that those who use this text will be inspired by their own creative impulses and expand the modest beginning that I have made here.

It is important to note that I do not consider myself a research social scientist. I claim no definite conclusions about what any group feels or thinks. The thrust of my presentations is deliberately biased to evoke reactions, and in this regard, the "data" I have presented in Chapter 3 may be viewed as unscientific or scientifically inconsequential. I suggest that its value lies more in the universality of its evocations—the common range of impressions, observations, thoughts, and speculations among the various populations—which in the end strives to provide a "way of seeing" that yields consolation and builds strength. To paraphrase a conversation with my colleague and mentor Robert Coles—no percentages, no statistics, no all-out conclusions. But there are many rewards, those any person recognizes when he or she feels newly educated by another human being. I am grateful for the expanded visions, the subtleties and specifics, and the multiplicity of undefinable truths that my participants—students of all ages, teachers, counselors, patients, and family members—have shared with me. They have been pushing me to "get something down" for others to use. It is to them that I am most indebted.

I must particularly thank Sandy Marks, Jr., anatomist and humanist in the Department of Cell Biology at the University of Massachusetts Medical School. Without Sandy's support and encouragement, my program would never have found a place in the medical school curriculum, nor would it have been permitted to evolve as it has to meet the needs of UMass students.

There are so many others I must acknowledge: colleagues who challenged me to bring my teaching style into the medical arena, special friends who encouraged me to blend psychology and the arts, and editors Hannelore Wass and Ron Wilder who envisioned the contribution such a book would make to the field of death education. My administrative assistant, Rita Wahle, and Carolyn Baker of Hemisphere participated in the mammoth task of obtaining copyright permissions and were masterful in tracking down copyright holders, publishers, and art galleries long defunct. For helping me translate my teaching into written form, I must especially thank Roberta Halporn, Director of the Center for Thanatology and Research in New York and Anthony Compagnone Jr., a medical student whose brilliance, precision, and joy in getting it right with words is a preamble to how he will be in patient care. I would be proud to have him as physician. And then there is my family: my dear children with whom I fought for computer time and who sat through interminable double-slide "rehearsals"; and my husband Richard, who, thankfully, has been as immersed in his design and sculpture as I have been in my book.

Finally, I feel especially blessed to have been able to create a "life work" out of two of my passions—teaching and art. Undoubtedly there will be purists who find my approach to art exploitative and utilitarian. In my own defense, I must say that I, too, appreciate "art for art's sake." At the same time, however, I believe that art has a purpose: to challenge, educate, and inspire. And it is in the struggle to understand art by filtering it through our own experience that we pay greatest tribute to the artist.

Sandra L. Bertman

1
Establishing the Perspective

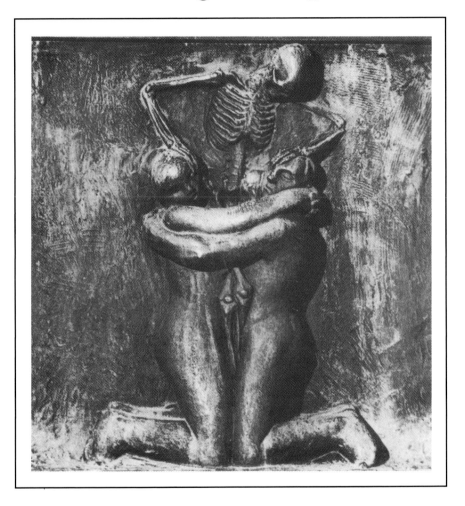

The age-old struggle between death and love: which is triumphant?

Figure 1. *Death Separating Man and Woman* (1906), Gustav Viegland. Bronze relief. Viegland Park, Oslo, Norway.

Chapter 1
Establishing the Perspective

The word death is not pronounced in New York, in Paris, in London because it burns the lips. The Mexican, in contrast, is familiar with death, jokes about it, caresses it, sleeps with it, celebrates it; it is one of his favorite toys and his most steadfast loves.

Octavio Paz[1]

Newspapers and television bombard our senses daily with reports of violence, accidents, AIDS, and the threat of megadeath. For some, death may occur suddenly from an accident, a heart attack, or a stroke. Most of us, however, will experience death slowly and in our later years. We are an increasingly aging population, and today (accidents and AIDS excluded) elderly persons hold a virtual monopoly on death. Many of us will develop chronic illnesses that will eventually prove fatal. Death will be protracted and will involve a growing awareness that we are, indeed, dying.

Yet our society seems insulated from and uncomfortable with the subject of death. The modern age has created a veritable "pornography of death,"[2] which extends even to disposition of the body. Aspects of the funeral industry have become exploitative, ostentatious, and sanitized. In hospital and nursing home settings—places where dying and death are daily events—mutual conspiracies of silence and closed communication patterns entered into by dying patients and staff are commonplace. Even children learn to collude in this game by concealing knowledge of their own impending deaths from their parents and medical personnel. Family ties have disintegrated, while the aged and dying have become segregated from their loved ones through consignment to nursing homes and institutional care. America might thus be characterized as a death-denying society.

There is no doubt that recent advances in medical technology have increased longevity—what gerontologists call "prolongevity." But along with major improvements in the technological aspects of care (e.g., marvelous devices for emergency services, ventilators, artificial kidneys, organ transplants) comes a myriad of ethical and humanistic dilemmas relating not only to where and when we die but also about the *way* we die. One of the paradoxes that has resulted from the evolution of medical science in recent decades is that the complexities involved in the treatment of illness

3

and disease often act as a barrier between the caregiver and the sick person. Highly technical diagnostic and therapeutic interventions can become obstacles to effective communication and treatment and accentuate the shift even farther away from close personal involvement with patients. Despite greater public sophistication and understanding of disease and despite changing social values and expectations on the part of patients and their families, certain truths about the impact of terminal illness remain fundamental. Illness is a profound experience that alters not only the emotional status quo but also behaviors and perceptions. Sick and injured persons are often frightened, anxious, depressed, guilty, ashamed, and angry.

Ignorance or misunderstanding by the caregiver of the emotional impact and spiritual ramifications of illness is unforgivable. Failure to appreciate the nature of suffering can result in medical and personal interventions that, although technically adequate, not only fail to relieve suffering but also become sources of pain and anxiety.

A story-essay, "Dying in Academe," which has proven evocative in my medical school teaching, makes us acutely aware of the incompatibility of these essential issues with the practice in today's teaching hospitals. Witnessing the intubation and unsuccessful resuscitation attempt on a fellow patient, a 78-year-old man begs to be left alone:

> Listen doctor. I don't want to die with tubes sticking out all over me. I don't want that my children should remember their father that way. All my life I tried to be a mensch, you understand? All my life, I tried to live so I could hold my head up. Rich I wasn't, but I managed to put my sons through college. I wanted to be able to hold my head up, to have dignity, even though I didn't have much money and didn't speak good English. Now I'm dying. O.K. I'm not complaining, I'm old and tired and have seen enough of life, believe me. But I still want to be a man, not a vegetable that someone comes and waters every day—not like him.[3]

Although a competent adult, the patient's expressed wishes are not honored; his was to be the most abhorrent fate: being coded (i.e., resuscitated at all costs). Ultimately he manages to disconnect himself from the mechanical apparatus, leaving a handwritten note for the physician: "Death is not the enemy, Doctor. Inhumanity is."

TERMINAL ILLNESS

Each of us is unique, a kaleidoscope of a particular set of experiences and beliefs. Accordingly, each of our deaths will be accompanied by its own host of associations and realities. Although the following dialogue on death focuses on living with terminal cancer, it is applicable to most chronic illnesses, including AIDS. The person with late-stage cancer frequently moves through a bewildering world of changing identities in which the disease and interactions with family members and the healthcare system can diminish the sense of fruitful living. Among the myriad issues dying persons must face, the following seem particularly salient:

1. communication difficulties between patient and medical staff and between patient and family;
2. uncomfortable psychological responses such as feelings of loneliness, vulnerability, alienation, and mutilation that, when repressed, produce a deep sense of suffering in the patient;
3. concern with dependency on others, which causes the patient to feel childlike and helpless, ashamed, and resentful;
4. a sense of loss of control over events in one's environment, which leads to a diminished sense of personal dignity and self-esteem;
5. concern with one's relationship to God or the hereafter and with existential issues such as the meaning and purpose of one's life.

INTERACTING WITH THE ARTS: WHY AND HOW

Good art, states E. J. Graff in *Sojourner*,[4] "can align our experiences, our feelings and our spirits so that we can grasp what is happening to us, so that we are neither lost in the intellectual coming from our mouths nor driven toward violence or frightened isolation by inexplicable waves of feeling." When "what is happening to us" involves confronting death—our own or another's—images from the visual and literary arts and from popular culture can stimulate insight, dialogue, solace, and even resolution. Employed with patience and sensitivity, these images can elicit responses and attitudes toward death heretofore unspoken or acknowledged even to ourselves. The very act of naming our worst fears is a step toward mastery and a sense of control. Often simply articulating such unmentionables is enough to initiate the painful but necessary work of grief. Furthermore, the discovery that we are already acquainted with the universal language of human suffering and therefore connected to the experience of others in different cultures and eras is itself consoling.

The humanities, literature and the arts, are resources relatively untapped by death educators and clinicians. The backbone of science is logic and experiment: that of art, intuition, and insight. The arts uncover realities that lie outside the quantifiable or statistically measurable. They invite us into the world of dying persons in a manner different from but no less penetrating than scientific analysis.

The following pages describe an educational process for using visual and literary images of illness and death to elicit personal feelings and reactions to dying and grief. This method of instruction can be used in almost any setting with almost any kind of group, regardless of age, level of education, or profession. The responses of five diverse groups to a slide presentation using images from the arts are provided to demonstrate the way that art binds us together in the universal experience of death. In addition, this book offers exercises and guidelines that can be used by teachers and counselors in any environment to achieve comparable results.

The primary emphasis of the approach presented here is the process rather than the product. Didactic lectures or documentary training films, even though focused on humanistic issues, usually challenge perceptions and beliefs on abstract or intellectual levels. Indeed, the problem of the distant and uninvolved professional, family member, or friend is compounded when the focus remains theoretical or passive as classroom or solo exercises often tend to be. Although the physician in "Dying in Academe" was familiar with the ethical principles of autonomy and informed consent and knew intellectually that a competent adult has the right to refuse treatment even if such a decision leads to death, her training led her to deny those rights to her patient.

Not only what one thinks (or ought to think) but observing what one does, feels, and intends, is relevant. Identifying and sharing perceptions with other colleagues and peers is crucial. If to relate on a person-to-person level is of paramount importance, then the atmosphere in which this is possible must be created and incorporated into formal teaching structures.

Death is always "center stage" for the physician, either as a harbinger of the patient's eventual demise or as a spectre of his own mortality.

Figure 2.
Death and the Physician
(1545), Hans Holbein.
Woodcut. From *Devils,
Demons, Death, and
Damnation* (1971),
Dover Publications.

Accordingly, this presentation of images and the interactive components employed to stimulate dialogue about death is aimed at increasing understanding of the psychosocial, ethical, cultural, and spiritual aspects of terminal illness and at providing opportunities for self-awareness and values clarification. The approach demonstrated here should help to accomplish the following:

1. increase understanding of psychosocial and existential issues related to death, dying, and grief in medical and lay populations;
2. stimulate more sensitive observations of the human condition by studying the visual and literary arts;
3. provide an arena for the generation of creative options and problem-solving possibilities for patients, family members, and healthcare professionals;
4. suggest alternatives in and additional resources for medical ethics education and patient care;
5. encourage new alliances between the medical community, other proponents of human services and the arts.

Tolstoy put it aptly when he wrote, "The business of art lies just in this . . . to make that understood and felt which in the form of an argument, might be incomprehensible and inaccessible. Usually it seems to the recipient of a truly artistic impression that he knew the thing before but had been unable to express it."[5] The literary and artistic images that follow, I hope, will provide many new outlets for self-expression and comforting avenues toward personal and professional self-knowledge.

NOTES

1. From Octavio Paz, Mexican poet and critic, source unknown.
2. From "The Pornography of Death" by Geoffrey Gorer, *Death, Grief and Mourning,* 1965, New York: Doubleday.
3. From "Dying in Academe" by Nancy L. Caroline, *The New Physician,* Nov. 1972, 655–657.
4. From *Sojourner* by E. J. Graff, October 1984, Cambridge, MA: Sojourner.
5. From *What is Art?* (1898), by L. Tolstoy, 1932, London: Oxford University Press.

REFERENCES

Bluebond-Langner, M. (1978). *The private words of dying children* (pp. 198–210). Princeton, NJ: Princeton University Press.

Callahan, D. (1987). *Setting limits.* New York: Simon & Schuster.

Engelhardt Jr., T. (1975, June). *A demand to die,* Hastings Center Report (p. 10). Briarcliff Manor, NY.

Feifel, H. (1977). *New meanings of death* (pp. 4–11). New York: McGraw-Hill.

Fulton, R. (1976). *Death and identity* (pp. 38–172). Bowie, MD: The Charles Press Publishers.

Gert, B., & Culver, C. (1979). The justification of paternalism. In W. Robison and M. Pritchard (Eds.). *Medical responsibility: Paternalism, informed consent, and euthanasia* (pp. 1–14). Clifton, NJ: Humana Press.

Glaser, B. G., & Strauss, A. L. (1966). *Awareness of dying.* Chicago: Aldine Publishing.

Hinton, J. (1963, January). The physical and mental distress of the dying. *Quarterly Journal of Medicine* 32, 1–21.

Leviton, D. (1991). *Horrendous death, health, and well-being.* Washington, DC: Hemisphere Pub. Corp.

Krant, M. J. (1974). *The dignity of death.* Springfield, IL: Thomas.

Mitford, J. (1963). *The American way of death.* New York: Simon & Schuster.

Parkes, C. M. (1972, but 1986 edition). *Bereavement: Studies of grief in adult life.* Madison, Connecticut: International Universities Press.

Pine, V. R. (1972). Death, dying, and social behavior. In B. Schoenberg, A. Carr, D. Peretz, and A. Kutscher (Eds.), *Anticipatory grief* (pp. 31–47). New York: Columbia University Press.

Rando, T. A. (1988). *Grieving.* Lexington, MA: Lexington Books.

Ross, E. K. (1969). *On death and dying.* New York: Macmillan Press.

Schoenberg, B., & Senescu, R. (1970). The patient's reaction to fatal illness. In B. Schoenberg, A. Carr, D. Peretz, and A. Kutscher (Eds.), *Loss and grief: Psychological management in medical practice* (pp. 162–172). New York: Columbia University Press.

Senescue, R. (1969, December). The problem of establishing communication with the seriously ill patient. *Annals of the New York Academy of Sciences* 164, 698–706.

Strauss, A. (1969, December). The family and staff during the last weeks and days of a terminal illness. *Annals of the New York Academy of Sciences* 164, 698–706.

Weisman, A. D. (1972). *On dying and denying. A psychiatric study of terminality.* New York: Behavioral Publications.

Weisman, A. D. (1984, 1986). *The coping capacity on the nature of being mortal.* New York: Human Sciences Press.

Weisman, A. D. (1970). Psychosocial considerations in terminal care. In B. Schoenberg, A. Carr, D. Peretz, and A. Kutscher (Eds.), *Loss and grief: Psychological management in medical practice.* New York: Columbia University Press.

Weisman, A. D., & Kastenbaum, R. (1968). *The psychological autopsy: A study of the terminal phase of life.* New York: Behavioral Publications.

Worden, J. W. (1982). *Grief counseling and grief therapy.* New York: Springer Publishing Company.

2
Images: Facing Death

The paradox of death personified: inviting yet forbidding, liberating yet all controlling.

Figure 3. *Portrait of Death* (1987), Benny Andrews. Oil and collage on canvas, 50 × 25. Courtesy of the artist.

Chapter 2

Images: Facing Death

The group leader, teacher, or counselor first prepares a series of slides or reproductions of art works and excerpts from poetry or fiction that present multiple attitudes toward the subject at hand. The topic could be violent or catastrophic death, disenfranchised grief, euthanasia or any one of the dimensions of the chronic or terminal illness experience: giving bad news, communication skills, helping children cope, disability, aging, bereavement, and the like.

In this instance I have selected images from a before-death presentation. Gleaned from the visual and literary classical and popular arts, the images are organized according to the following themes:

Theme   I: The Art of Dying: The Chosen Death
Theme II: Death and Afterlife: Views of Mortality and Immortality
Theme III: Far Worse than the Tumor: Existential Aloneness
Theme IV: Autonomy, Loss of Control, Unmentionable Feelings, Grief
Theme V: Tolerance for Ambivalence: The Land of the Sick versus the Land of the Well
Theme VI: The Moment of Death
Epilogue: The Birds of Sorrow: A Coexistence

The overall selection and organization of the images, presented in double-slide juxtapositions to maximize the opportunity for comparison, contrast, and aesthetics, is governed by the following three criteria:

1. relevance to or statement of concerns identified in the clinical literature;
2. evocative potential—that is, their ability to elicit participants' personal feelings rather than their intellectual, clinical, or rational reactions;
3. implicit humanistic bias. The images are intended to help participants identify their own concerns and beliefs and to enhance understanding, tolerance, compassion, and adaptive skills.

Insofar as possible I have arranged the visuals on the same page as corresponding textual material. The reader should refer frequently to the numbered illustrations while perusing the discussion, allowing for size restraints and lack of color.

Theme I
The Art of Dying: The Chosen Death

Figure 5. *The Death of Socrates* (1787), Jacques Louis David. Oil on canvas, 51 × 77¼. Metropolitan Museum of Art, New York, Wolfe Fund, 1931.

All my life I tried to be a mensch. . . . I still want to be a man, not a
vegetable that someone comes and waters every day.

Caroline, *Dying in Academe*

The ideal death scenario—that is, the death we would orchestrate for ourselves—is the focus of this section. Avery Weisman's (1970) definition of an "appropriate death," the living will, and ethical and spiritual attitudes toward suicide and euthanasia are relevant concepts.

By these criteria, the characteristics of such an ideal death seem to be timeliness, painlessness, consciousness, and preparedness. Death would come in later years; it would not be premature. We would be in control of our faculties, alert, and able to communicate. The occasion would not occur suddenly but rather eventually, with time for both philosophical and emotional preparation. We would be able to speak last words and receive the responsive farewells.

> *Later,*
> *when you face old age and its natural conclusion*
> *your courage will still be shown in the little ways,*
> *each spring will be a sword you'll sharpen,*
> *those you love will live in a fever of love,*
> *and you'll bargain with the calendar*
> *and at the last moment*
> *when death opens the back door*
> *you'll put on your carpet slippers*
> *and stride out.*

Figure 4.   Excerpt from "Courage." Anne Sexton. *The Awful Rowing Toward God.* Copyright 1975 by Loring Conant, Jr., Executor of the Estate of Anne Sexton. Reprinted by permission of Houghton Mifflin Company, Boston, and Sterling Lord Literistic, Inc., New York.

Anne Sexton captures in poetry the splendor of the timely demise (Figure 4), while David's classical painting, *Death of Socrates* (Figure 5), offers a visual interpretation of this ideal death. Socrates is presented just before he is to drink the hemlock that will kill him. Although late in years, the philosopher epitomizes vigor, stoicism, and decisiveness in his stance.

Detail of *The Death of Socrates* (See page 15).

His death is the ultimate expression of virtue; the laying down of one's life for the defense of ideals. The beloved teacher is surrounded by his grieving family, students, and jailer. His finger gestures heavenward, probably indicating his resolve or perhaps the path his soul will take, but a cancer patient in one of the seminars has suggested another interpretation: "giving God the finger."

Dying the good death also means being spiritually prepared. *The Goodman on his Deathbed* (Figure 6), a 15th-century woodcut illustration for *Ars Moriendi*, is another classic example of dignity and composure in the face of death. Intended for devotional use, this picture-sermon serves to remind the pious they need not fear the tortures of hell and damnation and that the next life offers a far more promising abode than the present one. Being confessed and absolved is virtual assurance of admission to heaven. The elements of the art of dying well are detailed in the woodcut: the monk administers the last rites to the Christian whose thoughts are of Christ and His saintly entourage. The angel receiving the soul leaving through the dying man's breath in the form of a small, naked praying figure completes the scenario, which has the devils enraged. Their utterances, literally inscribed, translate: "I am dumbfounded"; "This is no comfort"; "I am raging"; "We are disgraced"; "We have lost this soul."

Figure 6. *The Goodman on his Deathbed* (1471), Anonymous. Woodcut. Illustration from German Bibliotheque des Arts Decoratifs, Paris. Blockbook edition of *Ars Moriendi*, Bibliotheque des Arts Decoratifs, Paris.

> I ask for a natural death,
> no teeth on the ground,
> no blood about the place . . .
> It's not death I fear,
> but unspecified, unlimited pain.

Figure 7. "Death of a Critic." *Day by Day.* Robert Lowell (1977). Farrar, Straus and Giroux, New York.

Poet Robert Lowell asks for a nonviolent, "natural" death: no agony, no blood and guts, no bombs or bullets, "no teeth on the ground, no blood about the place"; it is not death he fears but "unspecified, unlimited pain" (Figure 7). Other examples are the closure and quiet dignity captured in Ralph W. Robinson's photograph *Fading Away* (Figure 8) and the clean and graceful dying exhibited in Sarah Bernhardt's portrayal of Camille's death (Figure 9), a marvelously bloodless, beautifully melodramatic scene.

Figure 8. *Fading Away* (1859), Ralph W. Robinson. Composite photograph made from five negatives. Courtesy of Royal Photographic Society, London.

Figure 9. *Sarah Bernhardt Playing Camille* (1880), Courtesy of the International Museum of Photography at George Eastman House, Rochester, NY.

In contrast, the unreconciled, painful scene suggested by the contemporary Beckmann painting, *Large Death Scene* (Figure 10), markedly opposes the peaceful leavetaking of the photographs, 15th century woodcut, and painting *The Death of Socrates*. The last moments of this man's death are undignified, unromanticized, unbeautiful. There is no sense of composure, control, or communication. Rather, this expressionist work lays bare the indignity that can befall a person whose dying is prolonged. Raw,

Figure 10.   *Grosse Sterbeszene (Large Death Scene)* (1906), Max Beckmann. Oil on canvas, 131,4 × 141 cm. Besitzer, Bayer Staatsgemaldesammlungen.

Figure 11. Detail of *AIDS Patient* (1989), Luis Cruz Azaceta. Acrylic on canvas, 48 × 36. Courtesy of Frumkin/Adams Gallery, New York.

naked agony is portrayed by the dying man's postures and by those witnessing his demise. Compare the stark isolation and technological imprisonment underscored by the detail from Luis Cruz Azaceta's *AIDS Patient* (Figure 11).

To guard against such ugly scenarios, JoAnn Kelley Smith, author of *Free Fall*, makes a "covenant" with her physician about truth-telling, pain and suffering, and the prolongation of life (Figure 12). Understanding her decision, he promises to honor her dignity. Her covenant is, in essence, the "Living Will" legislation (Figure 13), wherein the *will* of the patient, not the *health* of the patient, is supreme law.

Voluntary deaths have been omitted from this presentation because the focus might shift to suicide. Though the concept is also apropos of David's work, Socrates was sentenced to die by the State; the

Then I asked him to make a covenant with me:
that he would always tell me the truth,
that he would not allow me to suffer,
and that he would not use
heroic methods to keep me alive.
He promised, "You will be able to die
with a feeling of dignity."

Figure 12. *Free Fall.* JoAnn Kelley Smith. (1975). Reprinted by permission of Judson Press, Valley Forge, PA.

If the time comes when I can no longer take part in decisions for my own future, let this statement stand as the testament of my wishes.

If there is no reasonable expectation of my recovery from physical or mental or spiritual disability, I _____ request that I be allowed to die and not be kept alive by artificial means or heroic measures.

Death is as much a reality as birth, growth, maturity and old age—it is the one certainty. I do not fear death as much as I fear the indignity of deterioration, dependence and hopeless pain. I ask that drugs be mercifully administered to me for terminal suffering even if they hasten the moment of death.

Figure 13. From the *Living Will,* Concern for Dying. Prepared by the Euthanasia Educational Council, New York, 34th printing, (rev. April 1974).

method of execution happened to be suicide. But were one not aware of the historical context, the scene could evoke the hospice philosophy. Substitute a Brompton's cocktail (morphine) for the hemlock and a volunteer or nurse for the jailer, who is participating along with family and friends, and one is witness to a "perfect" hospice death. As in an image created by a bereavement coordinator, all are clearly involved, in accord, and moved by the event (Figure 14).

Figure 14. *Bereavement Coordinator* (1990), Hospice of Cheshire County, New Hampshire.

Theme II
Death and Afterlife: Views of Mortality and Immortality

Figure 31. *L'enterrement de Casagemas (Evocation, The Burial of Casagemas)*, AMVP 1131, (1901), Pablo Picasso. Oil on canvas, 59¹/8 × 35¹/2. Reproduced by permission of Ville de Paris, Musée d'Art Moderne, Paris.

23

Death is not extinguishing the light. It is putting out the lamp because dawn has come.

Tagore (1937)

The living will represents an expression of the belief that pain and indignity on earth can be worse than death. Yet some living beings— human or otherwise—are not so anxious to migrate to the hereafter, to claim their peaceful reward in the great beyond. The cartoon of two clams conversing is an example of this attitude (Figure 16).

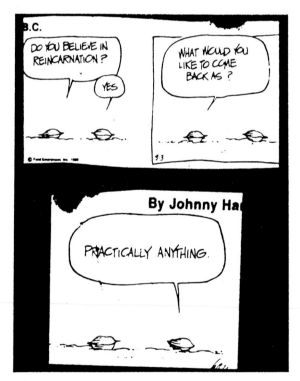

Figure 16. "Two Clams Conversing," from *B.C.* (1980), Johnny Hart. By permission of Johnny Hart and Creators Syndicate, Los Angeles, CA.

E. E. Cummings also sees death as the worst state imaginable. In his poem, "dying is fine)but Death," he develops the thesis not only through imagery but also through syntax, especially through parts of speech (Figure 15). Dying is an active verb, "lively," living, if you will. Death, a noun, is final, legal, even evil. The poem concludes with a prayer to God for forgiveness for the "sin" of death.

Filmmaker Woody Allen also expresses his views on nonexistence. He is not afraid of dying; he just doesn't want to be there when it happens. This 20th century philosopher sees death in worldly, life-as-usual terms. He wonders whether he will be able to change a $20 bill in the hereafter (Allen, 1971a), or, if the soul lives on without the body, whether his clothes will fit too loosely (Allen, 1971b). Although he claims he does not believe in an afterlife, he is, nevertheless, bringing a change of underwear. Allen sees death as the worst embarrassment. Juxtaposing the everyday nitty-gritty with the unknown, the profound with the petty as only his comic genius can, he manages to capture the existential anxiety shrouding the situation (Figure 17).

dying is fine)but Death

?o
baby
i

wouldn't like

Death if Death
were
good:for

when(instead of stopping to think)you

begin to feel of it,dying
's miraculous
why?be

cause dying is

perfectly natural;perfectly
putting
it mildly lively(but

Death

is strictly
scientific
& artificial &

evil & legal)

we thank thee
god
almighty for dying

(forgive us,o life!the sin of Death

Figure 15. "dying is fine)but Death." E. E. Cummings. *Xiape.* George James Firmage (Ed.). Reprinted by permission of Liveright Publishing Corp. Copyright 1950 by E. E. Cummings. Copyright 1979, 1978, 1973 by Nancy T. Andrews. Copyright 1979, 1973 by George James Firmage. World rights by permission of Grafton Books, a division of Harper Collins Publishers, Ltd., London.

**... The fear that there may be
no afterlife—a depressing
thought, particularly for those
who have bothered to shave;
also, there is a fear that there
is an afterlife but no one will
know where it is being held.**

Figure 17.   Woody Allen. (January 20, 1973). *The New Yorker.*

Emily Dickinson questions whether death, which dispossesses us of our flesh, is only the literal endpoint of a biologic process. Her poem postulates the argument in terms of two ranges of imagery (Figure 18*a*).

Death is a dialogue
between the spirit and the dust.
"Dissolve," says death.
The spirit, "Sir, I have another trust."

Figure 18 (*a*).   "Death is a dialogue/Between the spirit and the dust." Emily Dickinson. No. 976 from *The Poems of Emily Dickinson* (1979). T. Johnson (Ed.). Harvard University Press, Cambridge.

Epitaphs and the visual arts are less subtle in their depiction of the physical manifestations of death, drawing attention to the dissolution, deterioration, and smell of rotting flesh. An epitaph (Figure 19) illustrates

*He that was sweet to my repose
Now is a stink under my nose
This is said of me
Soon it will be said of thee*

Figure 19.   Epitaph: "He that was sweet to my repose/Now is a stink under my nose . . . ." (1710). Dr. Isaac Bartholomew, Cheshire, Connecticut.

the "message" of the *danse macabre*.[1] The image presented in the dance of death in 1510 is death personified: a fleshless skeleton that leads his partners to their deaths (Figure 20).

Other artists' versions depict the literal ravages of death. With painstaking realism, Otto Dix's rendition painted in 1924 on the same theme, *Dying Soldier*, exposes the decomposition of the decaying body (Figure 21). Even a fleshless skeleton would be company. A favorite illustration in this catalog of maggotry or the

Figure 20. *Death and Soldier* (1510), Albrecht Dürer. Woodcut. Museum of Art, Rhode Island School of Design, Providence. Gift of Mr. Henry D. Sharpe. Photography by Cathy Carver.

Figure 21. *Dying Soldier* (1924), Otto Dix. From *Der Kreig*, Etching and aquatint. Print collection, Miriam and Ira D. Wallach Division of Art, Prints and Photographs. The New York Public Library, Astor, Lenox and Tilden Foundations, New York.

conquering worm is the epitaph by Lord Byron for a carrier who died of drunkenness (Figure 22).

John Adams lies here, of the parish of Southwell,
A carrier who carried his can to his mouth well.
He carried so much and he carried so fast,
He could carry no more—so was carried at last;
For the liquor he drank being too much for one,
He could not carry off; so he's now carri-on.

Figure 22.   Lord Byron. Epitaph on John Adams of Southwell, a carrier who died of drunkenness, September 1807. From *Chronicles of the Tombs* (1857) a select collection of epitaphs by Thomas Pettigrew, Bohn's Standard Library, London.

In the second stanza of the Dickinson poem, death is described as a transition to a new state of being (Figure 18*b*). The spirit's final resting place is not trapped within the decomposed flesh, under the sod, or under the trees.

Death is a dialogue
between the spirit and the dust.
"Dissolve," says death.
The spirit, "Sir, I have another trust."

Death doubts it, argues from the ground
The spirit turns away
Just laying off, for evidence,
An overcoat of clay.

Figure 18 (*b*).   "Death is a dialogue/Between the spirit and the dust." Emily Dickinson. No. 976 from *The Poems of Emily Dickinson* (1979). T. Johnson (Ed.). Harvard University Press, Cambridge.

Figure 23. Epitaph: "Under the sod and under the trees/Here lies the body of Solomon Pease/The Pease are not here/There's only the pod/The Pease shelled out and went to God." Source unknown.

Figure 24. Epitaph: "Here lyeth Sara Young, Who went to sleep with Christ." January 6, 1741.

In the epitaph of Solomon Pease (Figure 23), the Pease have left the pod, so to speak, "shelled out" and gone to God. Sara Young's epitaph (Figure 24) implies separation from earthly remains and joining ("going to sleep with") Christ. El Greco painted *Burial of Count Orgaz* (Figure 25) on the chapel wall marking the place where the count's body was interred. The artist poises Orgaz's soul, a small, swaddled figure midway on the wall, halfway between the earth and heavenly realms, while being escorted by an angel to meet with Christ, the Virgin Mary, and Peter. Compare this imagery still again with that of the 15th century woodcut *The Goodman on his Deathbed* (Figure 6).

At every point in history and in every culture people appear to be concerned with the moment of death, the body reft of its spirit and the journey to the afterlife. William Blake portrays the soul as a gentle female form reluctantly and lovingly leaving the body (Figure 26). The Egyptian soulbird, "ba," hovers to protect and accompany the being to the otherworld (Figure 27). In an Indian Hare Krishna version, the soul leaves the body at each developmental stage of life, moving into different shells (baby, young man, middle age, old man) like a hermit crab, until it fuses, ultimately, in the otherworld with the Eternal One (Figure 28).

Figure 25. *Burial of Count Orgaz* (1586), El Greco. Oil on canvas, 16′ × 11′10 Church of St. Thomas, Toledo.

Figure 26. *Illustrations to the Grave* (1808), William Blake. Cadell and Davies, Strand Publishers, London.

Figure 28. Hare Krishna door-to-door circular. Undated.

Figure 27. *Papyrus of Ani* (1500 B.C.), Egypt. Reproduced by courtesy of the Trustees of the British Museum, London.

The ideal resting place is not always depicted in traditional Biblical terms—resting in the bosom of Abraham (Figure 29) or being received by Christ in a heaven of eternal life populated by saints and martyrs. Nor is it universal. A 19th-century painting (Figure 30) in a Buddhist temple of the Tibetan afterlife portrays completion and everlasting bliss in terms of a suggestive fusion, a sexual union with one's Yidam, the projection of one's higher mind or higher self. In *Evocation, The Burial of Casagemas* (Figure 31),

Figure 30.   *Tibetan Afterlife* (19th century). Fosco Maraini Collection, Florence. Central figure is Samantabhadra with his consort.

Figure 29.   *The Blessed and the Damned*, miniature from the *Psautier de Saint Louis and Blanche of Castile* (c. 1223–30). Ms. Latin 1186, Fol. 171. Bibliothèque Nationale, Paris.

Figure 31. (See page 23).

Picasso memorializes his friend, Casagemas, mounting a horse, cavorting with lushly stockinged nude ladies of the spheres, acting out, perhaps, unfulfilled earthly sexual fantasies. His body is mourned below in this world in 1901, much like Count Orgaz's in 1586.

There are many renditions of personal reunion in afterlife: the Pigeons (Figure 32); the Carpenters (Figure 33); the joined hands on the tombstone in a cemetery in Ars-en Re, France (Figure 34); the ballad "Barbara Allen," the lovers' song, "somewhere . . . there's a place for us," from *West Side Story* (Bernstein, 1918); the Pyramus and Thisbe myth; in *Romeo and*

Figure 32.   Old couple, sculpture on tombstone. Famille de Pigeon, cemetery in France.

Carpenter

Louella 1852–1949
William 1852–1947

Lovely and pleasant
in their lives
in death they were not divided

Figure 33.   Epitaph: "Lovely and pleasant/in their lives/in death they were not divided, Louella Carpenter 1852-1949; William Carpenter 1852-1947."

Juliet (Shakespeare, 1595). It makes perfect sense to an 8-year-old youngster that his grandparents would simply want to be together in the afterlife to continue their card games (Figure 35).

Emily Dickinson's poem (Figures 18*a* and *b*) frames two points of view fleshed out by the previous montage of images: (1) death is literal annihilation and separation, and (2) death is literal relief from the suffering and torments of this earth. Witness the Negro spiritual, "All my trials, Lord, will soon be over," and the Living Will.

Figure 34.   Clasped hands on a tomb in Ars-en Re cemetery. Courtesy of the Photographer, Anne de Brunhoff.

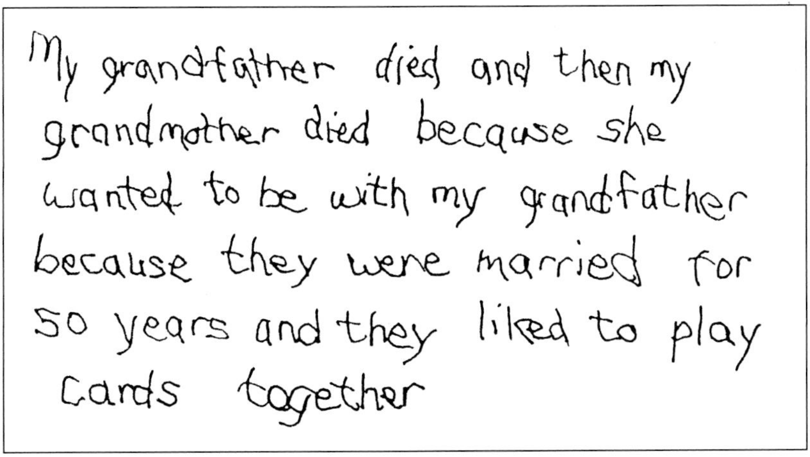

My grandfather died and then my grandmother died because she wanted to be with my grandfather because they were married for 50 years and they liked to play cards together

Figure 35.   Sandra Bertman. (1972). Equinox Collection, "Death: A Primer for All Ages," collection of Images, Newton, MA. In *Death: A Primer for All Ages* (1990). The Center for Thanatology Research and Education, New York.

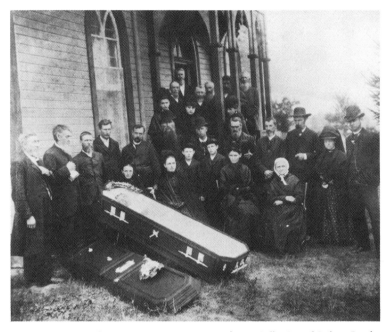

Figure 36.   Funeral Scene (c. 1850), Muncie, Indiana. Collection of Robert Reed.

Robert Jay Lifton's work (1961) adds another slant to the "overcoat of clay" metaphor. Death is transcended not by personal immortality—the idea of another world where one's body or soul lives on forever—but by what one leaves behind in the world. Lifton identifies five modes of symbolic immortality. One lives on (1) biologically, through one's children, family, tribe, clan; (2) theologically, as we have seen, in an afterlife with one's God; (3) creatively, through one's work, painting, poetry, scientific or philanthropic contribution, deed; (4) naturally, through a reincorporation with the elements; or (5) transcendentally, through an experiential or psychological sense of escaping time and space.

Artistic and literary depictions of these modes of symbolic immortality abound. The more obvious ones, biological and theological, can be visualized through intergenerational photographs (Figure 36) or the previously mentioned depictions of afterlife reunions with Christ (Figures 6, 23–25), Abraham (Figure 29), or the Tibetan Yidam (Figure 30). A lovely phrasing of creative immortality is Auden's epitaph to the poet Yeats (Figure 37), and a sculptural parallel exists in Michelangelo's *Pieta* (Figure 38).

Earth, receive an honored guest;
William Yeats is laid to rest;
Let the Irish vessel lie
emptied of its poetry.

Figure 37. "In memory of W. B. Yeats." W. H. Auden. *Verse III, Collected Shorter Poems, 1927–1957* (1966). Farber & Farber Limited, London.

Figure 38. *Pieta* (1498), Michelangelo. St. Peter's Basilica, Rome.

A combination of the biological and the creative, or transcendental (what Hans Morganthal (1961) defines as a social immortality) can be found in the Talmud:

> When the Rabbis asked: "Why does the Bible in recording David's death say 'And David slept with his fathers?' Why does it not say 'And David died'?" The sages replied, "because David left a son who walked in the good ways of his father, and who continued his noble deeds; therefore, David was really not dead but lived on through the good deeds of his son." [Baba Batra 116a.]

Figure 39. *Christmas Morning* (1944), Andrew Wyeth. Tempera, 23³/4 × 38³/4 in. Photo courtesy of the Wyeth Collection. © Andrew Wyeth.

The natural and transcendental modes of immortality are depicted by Andrew Wyeth's *Christmas Morning* (Figure 39) or by Paul Klee's *St. Francis* (1933) in which the figure literally merges into the landscape both in color and line. In these works, the cemetery becomes a kind of nursery for the perpetuation of the natural life cycle. The Norwegian artist Edvard

Munch didn't want anyone to bring flowers to his grave. He explained, "From my rotting body, flowers shall grow, and I shall be in them" (Maze, 1990). Speaking of death and decay, poet Alice Walker reminds us, "It hardly matters/Which/Since both are on the way, maybe—to becoming daffodils" (Walker, 1968). From popular culture, a lyric from the musical *Oklahoma* expounds the same consolation, though slightly tongue-in-cheek: "The daisies in the dell/Give off a different smell/Because poor Jud is underneath the ground" (Rodgers & Hammerstein, 1943).

In the transcendental mode of immortality, the spirit finds ultimate fulfillment in the death of the body. John Burroughs expresses a philosophy that extols the absoluteness of spirit and a peaceful sense of relationship between the personal and the infinite (Figure 40).

I shall not be imprisoned in that grave where you are to bury my body. I shall be diffused in great nature, in the soil, in the air, in the sunshine, in the hearts of those who love me.

Figure 40.   John Burroughs. American poet (1837–1921). Source unknown.

The donation of an organ or a body to scientific research—the anatomical gift (Figure 41)—is another example of the concept of transcendental immortality. The deathbed is viewed rather as a lifebed, an altar of selflessness upon which the donor continues to nurture, educate, and relieve the suffering of those he leaves behind.

Give my kidneys to one who depends on a machine to exist. Take my bones, every muscle, every fiber and nerve in my body and find a way to make a crippled child walk. Explore every corner of my brain. Take my cells, if necessary, and let them grow so that someday a speechless boy will shout at the crack of a bat and a deaf girl will hear the sound of rain against her window.

Burn what is left of me and scatter the ashes to the wind to help the flowers grow. If you must bury something, let it be my faults, my weaknesses, and all prejudice against my fellow man.

If, by chance, you wish to remember me, do it with a kind deed or word to someone who needs you. If you do all I have asked, I will live forever.

Figure 41.   Robert N. Test. "Give my kidneys . . . ." In Ann Landers column, *The Boston Globe*, February 1978. Reproduced by permission of Ann Landers and Creators Syndicate.

Theme III
Far Worse than the Tumor: Existential Aloneness

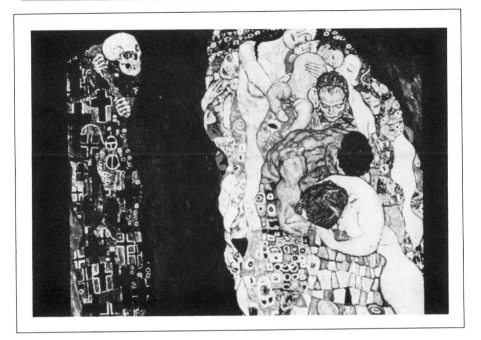

Figure 42. *Death and Life* (1911, rev. 1915), Gustav Klimpt. Oil on canvas, 178 × 146 cm. Private collection, Vienna.

Parting is all we know of heaven, and all we need of hell.

Emily Dickinson

Regardless of how one dies or how one views being dead, death means separation not only from the flesh but also from the human community. Gustav Viegland's bronze relief of the clinging lovers being separated by death (Figure 1) is a superb counterpart to the Emily Dickinson epigraph. Gustav Klimpt's painting *Death and Life* (Figure 42), is a particularly apt speculation about the effects of death's invasion of a family. The skeletal figure of death stands quite apart from the group of intertwined figures, who cling physically and emotionally to one another. The better defined figure in the painting might represent Rusanoff, a character from Aleksander Solzhenitsyn's novel *Cancer Ward* (Figure 43), who feels abruptly divorced from his family and his life when he receives the diagnosis of cancer.

Figure 42. (See page 39).

But in a few days this whole close-knit, ideal Rusanoff Family—with two older and two younger children, with their completely well-ordered life and their spotless apartment, unstintingly furnished—had receded until it had vanished *on the other side of the tumor.* No matter what happened to the father, they were alive and would go on living. No matter how they might worry, exhibit concern, or weep now, *the tumor had divided him from them like a wall, and he remained alone on this side of it.*

Figure 43.   From *Cancer Ward.* Aleksander L. Solzhenitsyn (1968). Translated by Leo Gruliow. Doubleday, New York. (Italics added.)

The same sense of isolation and separation is expressed repeatedly in clinical literature, fiction, and film. In her autobiographical work, *The Woman Said Yes*, author Jessamyn West (1976) speculates that her own sister did not tell her about her first evening in the terminal ward, either because she couldn't believe it herself, or to spare West pain (Figure 44). In the short story "Slim," author Adam Mars-Jones (1988) also uses the imagery of separate worlds in the context of AIDS, ". . . getting Slim [what AIDS is called in Uganda] only involves being exiled from the young, the well, the real."

> *I didn't tell Grace about my first evening in the terminal ward, either because I couldn't believe it myself or to save her the pain. The sick soon come to understand that they live in a different world from the well and that the two cannot communicate.*

Figure 44. Excerpt from *The Woman Said Yes*, Copyright 1976 by Jessamyn West. Reprinted by permission of Harcourt Brace Jovanovich, Inc., Orlando, FL.

In the Japanese film *Ikiru*, the protagonist, Mr. Watanabe, exhibits "knowing," defined by Avery Weisman as "middle knowledge" (Figure 45).[2] When Watanabe's suspicions of his cancer diagnosis are confirmed

Figure 45. *Ikiru* (1960), Akira Kurosawa. From Donald Richie, *Films of Akira Kurosawa* (Rev. ed.). Copyright 1984 The Regents of the University of California.

through the nonverbal behavior of the physicians—despite their reassurances that he suffers only from an ulcer—the sound track cuts dramatically to total silence. In the Tolstoy novella *The Death of Ivan Ilyich* (Figure 46), the title character is tormented by a deceptive game of mutual pretense that the doctors and family force him to play.

> What tormented Ivan Ilyich most was the deception, the lie, which for some reason, they all accepted, that he was not dying but was simply ill, and that he only need keep quiet and undergo a treatment and then something very good would result.

Figure 46.   From *The Death of Ivan Ilyich*. Leo Tolstoy (1886). Translated by Rosemary Edmonds (Penguin Classics, 1960). Copyright 1960 by Rosemary Edmonds. Penguin Books, Ltd., London.

Cancer is a family affair—that is, the specter of death does not simply single out the one afflicted family member. It affects each of them. No one escapes unscathed. Everyone's nerves sit ceremoniously, precariously, balancing against "losing it" or "letting go."[3] Generally, we do not want to accept such a bitter fact. In the play *The Shadow Box*, Maggie, a woman who is unable to accept her husband's end-stage cancer, maintains this precarious balance by denying the reality of his prognosis. She engages in frenetic activity and banter despite his plea to acknowledge his impending death (Figure 47).

Joe   Come inside.

Maggie   What will we do in there?

Joe   Try . . . that's all, just try. Live with it; look at it. Don't make me do it alone.

Figure 47.   *The Shadow Box*. Michael Cristopher. Copyright 1979 by Michael Cristopher. Reprinted by permission of Samuel French, Inc., New York.

In the novel *Sunshine*, lover and friends are also unable to live with it, look at it, or listen to what the young woman needs to say about what she wants done with her baby, her precious legacy to those she cares about (Figure 48). In a Dylan Thomas poem (Figure 49), a son who might have unfinished business with his dying father is desperate for intimate involvement of any kind: a blessing or even a curse, anything that will perpetuate their connectedness. "Slap me. Hug me," begs the lover of his dying companion in the off-Broadway musical, *Falsettoland* (1990), giving a modern twist to Thomas's sentiment.

From the realm of popular culture, get-well cards illustrate our society's attitude of denial and aversion. Until quite recently the only message to be found in the store racks was the cheery "you'll be up on your feet and out of there in no time," obscenely inappropriate for the terminally ill. One card (Figure 50), the deadly accuracy of which is masked by humor, lays bare the reason for shunning the seriously ill. Statistics support this sad reality. It is common knowledge that the call lights of dying patients are answered last, and that once the terminal phase has set in, fewer and fewer doctors, staff members, family, and friends come to visit.

I think I have accepted death as well as anyone can. But what makes it hard is when I try to talk to people close to me and tell them what I'd like done—with Jill and Sam and my things. They refuse to listen and then I feel funny. It's such a hassle . . .

Figure 48. *Sunshine*. Norma Klein (1974). Avon Books, New York.

And you my father, there on that sad height
Curse, Bless me now with your fierce tears, I pray.
Do not go gentle into that good night.
Rage, rage against the dying of the light.

Figure 49. From "Do Not Go Gentle into that Good Night." Dylan Thomas. *Dylan Thomas: The Poems* (1971). J. M. Dent & Sons, Ltd., London.

Not only the patient, but also family members express feelings of alienation like Rusanoff in *Cancer Ward* (Figure 43). An article on the June 1990 AIDS pledge walk in Boston, "From All Walks of Life" (Diamant, 1990), points out this similarity between AIDS and cancer, cystic fibrosis, and a dozen other "awful" diseases. "Patients who suffer from malignancies with unfamiliar names *and* the families who sit by their bedsides also inhabit a separate sphere that feels totally isolated from and abandoned by the busy, healthy, apparently uncaring world."

Figure 50. "We all hate to see you sick." Gi-Gi Cards by Gallant Greeting Cards, Chicago, MCMLXXI 35GW-1103.

Why is it so difficult to associate with persons who are dying? Freud (1908) explains that our unconscious cannot face the thought of its own death. Even Freud, who first elucidated the phenomenon, death anxiety, reportedly told his wife, "If one of the two of us dies before the other, I think I'll move to Paris."

Another greeting card (Figure 51) echoes the *memento mori* message implicit in serious or fatal illness. If anything is contagious from the bedside of the dying, it is the intimation of our own mortality.

The awareness that we really mourn ourselves has little to do with chronological age. On the occasion of her grandfather's death, an eighth-grader realized that she, too, one day would be facing her own death. Her poem (Figure 52) also echoes Ivan Ilyich's frustration: the deceptive games played by doctors and family.

Figure 51. "Heavens, if nice people like you can get sick." Classique Studio Cards. Reprinted with permission of Gibson Greeting Cards, Inc., Cincinnati, OH 45237. All rights reserved. M730G6, 605C050-2.

My grandfather's gone—Never to return.
He was in the hospital getting better.
He died though I knew he would.
Grandma didn't cry. Her eyes were dry.
She kept saying "I wish I could cry."
She never cried. I didn't either
except when I thought
THIS will happen to ME too.

Figure 52. Poem. Eighth grader. Bertman Collection, Newton, MA. Reprinted in *Death: A Primer for All Ages* (1990). The Center for Thanatology Research and Education, New York.

Another way of preserving our sense of invulnerability, of distancing ourselves, is by finding reasons for the tragic fate. We fantasize that we are accountable for our illness and health. The patient is to blame. One must have done something to deserve the malady. Again, uncannily, our culture voices this attitude in another get-well card (Figure 53). The impli-

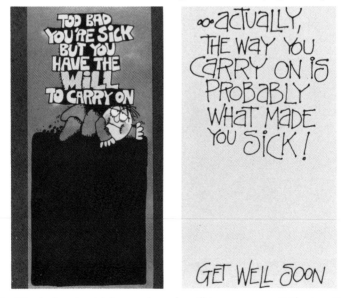

Figure 53. "Too bad you're sick but you have the will to carry on . . . ." Classique Studio Cards. Reprinted with permission of Gibson Greeting Cards, Inc., Cincinnati, OH 45237. All rights reserved. F264G 405C050-12.

cations are that one ate the wrong food, smoked too much, shared needles, engaged in dangerous sexual acts, took improper precautions, "waited too long to seek treatment" (Figures 54–57).

Figure 54. "Augustus Who Wouldn't Eat His Soup," Henrich Hoffman. In *Struwelpeter*, Frederick Warne & Co., Inc., New York.

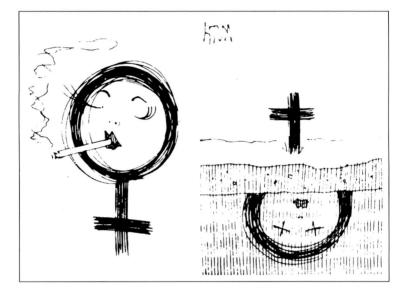

Figure 55. Cartoon: "Smoking Causes Death." *The Boston Globe,* unsigned, undated. On file in Bertman Collection.

Figure 56. Cartoon: "The real reason dinosaurs became extinct." (1982, 1984), Gary Larson. *The Far Side* Cartoon by Gary Larson is reprinted by permission of Chronical Features, San Francisco, CA.

Figure 57. "Protejase no se contamine. Evite el SIDA use condon" (1990). Courtesy Visual AIDS.

To the physician, dying patients present threats on two counts: they are messengers of *memento mori*, who remind the physician of personal annihilation; at the same time, they confront the physician with his or her own helplessness, with tangible proof of professional "failure" and the limitations of medicine (Figure 2). In *Cancer Ward* a physician retorts angrily to a patient who asks to read about his illness (Figure 58). In this context, a Modell cartoon can be viewed as a literal variation of the verbal slap (Figure 59).

Why you don't deserve to read it, if only because you neglected yourself like that. Why didn't you come to the hospital sooner? Why did you wait until they had to bring you here almost dead?

Figure 58. From *Cancer Ward*. Aleksander L. Solzhenitsyn (1968). Translated by Leo Gruliow. Doubleday, New York.

Figure 59. Cartoon: Physician spanking patient. A. B. Modell, source unknown. On file in Bertman Collection.

One type of therapeutic intervention asks the patient to look hard at the intrapsychic meaning of illness and to accept part of the responsibility for healing. Carl Simonton writes in *Getting Well Again* that he instructs cancer patients to answer five questions (Figure 60) in an effort to assume an active role in the healing process. Employing the same technique, Bernard Siegel (1986) in *Love, Medicine and Miracles* requires that the person abandon the passivity inherent in the connotation of the term, "patient,"

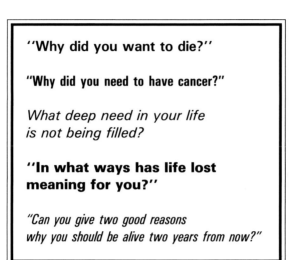

> "Why did you want to die?"
>
> "Why did you need to have cancer?"
>
> *What deep need in your life*
> *is not being filled?*
>
> **"In what ways has life lost**
> **meaning for you?"**
>
> *"Can you give two good reasons*
> *why you should be alive two years from now?"*

Figure 60. *Getting Well Again* (1978). Carl Simonton, Stephanie Matthews-Simonton, and James Creigton. J. P. Tarcher, Inc., Los Angeles.

becoming instead a responsible patient, a "res-pant," as if positive thinking or self-discipline is the first step to reverse the course of disease.

Not all writers have been taken in by these "self-help" theories. Susan Sontag's *Illness as Metaphor* (1977) offers a plethora of historical and literary accounts of persons who "contracted" their diseases by virtue of their personality characteristics. Cancer, for example, has been viewed as a disease of the repressed and passive. Sontag cites an Auden poem, "Miss Gee," in which a religious young woman held herself back from temptation and sexual fulfillment. The physician exhibits both closed communication and a blame-the-victim accusation in his relationship with the patient (Figure 61).

Doctor Thomas looks her over
And then he looked some more;
Walked over to his wash-basin,
Said, "Why didn't you come here before?"
● ● ●
"Childless women get it,
And men when they retire;
It's as if there had to be some outlet
For their foiled creative fire."

Figure 61. "Miss Gee." In *Collected Shorter Poems 1927–1957.* W. H. Auden (1966). Faber & Faber, Ltd., London.

Gruenwald's painting, *The Guilty Lovers* (Figure 62), is painfully appropriate today as a metaphor for those who believe risky sexual behaviors are the cause of AIDS. The very organs that have been the source of indulgence and pleasure are attacked by the snakes and vermin of death in this punishment-fits-the-crime portrayal. In this context, we might reconsider the get-well card, "If *nice* people like you can get sick . . . nobody's safe" (Figure 51). A way of distancing oneself from the inevitable dance macabre—at least for a while and a bit like whistling in the dark—is by believing that *they*, the "not-nice" people, get sick.

Viewing cancer as a disease of the failure of expressiveness, or the suggestion that the patient must have done something to deserve his or her fate, is blaming the victim. The original insult of the illness would be quite enough. Our judgment and condemnation is yet another affront to sustain. "Why me?" is a cry of pain or frustration, a plea for consolation, not explanation.

The term "victim" itself is problematic. Even the word "patient" is depersonalizing. So, too, is lumping people into groups: referring to them as the dying, the bereaved. All these terms tend to distance *us* from *them*. Only the very strongest can fight back by insisting on the use of respectful words in relation to their conditions. Compare and contrast the phrases

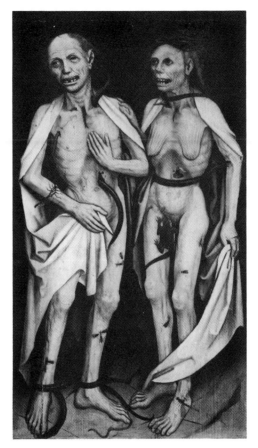

Figure 62. *Les Amants Trépassés (The Guilty Lovers)* (16th century), Mathias Gruenwald. Musée de l'Oeuvre Notre Dame de Strasbourg.

"AIDS victims" (substitute "cancer" or "Alzheimer's") and "person with AIDS" (PWA) or "persons living with AIDS" (PLWA). Again, leave it to fiction writers to debunk the latest acronyms and buzz words. The person with AIDS in the short story "Slim" tells the reader that he's a string of letters that he doesn't remember "except the first one's P and stands for person" (Mars-Jones, 1988). A brilliant use of humor as a coping mechanism is his witty conclusion that illness is making him "quite an internationalist: an African infection and some dated American slang."

Theme IV
Autonomy, Loss of Control, Unmentionable Feelings, Grief

Figure 64. *Gramp,* photographs (1976), Mark Jury and Dan Jury. Narrative text by Mark Jury, Grossman Publishers, A Division of The Viking Press, New York.

I do not fear death as much as I fear . . . dependence . . . .

Living Will

The loss of autonomy, independence, self-sufficiency, and the prospect of being literally disrobed are great sources of anguish for sick persons (or, for that matter, well persons). As relevant today as in 1886 are the sentiments of shame expressed by Tolstoy's protagonist, Ivan Ilyich (Figure 63). The special arrangements that had to be made for the protago-

For his excretions also special arrangements had to be made, and this was a torment to him every time—a torment from the uncleanliness, the unseemliness, and the smell, and from knowing that another person had to take part in it.

Figure 63. From *The Death of Ivan Ilyich.* Leo Tolstoy (1886). Translated by Rosemary Edmonds (Penguin Classics, 1960). Copyright 1960 by Rosemary Edmonds. Penguin Books, Ltd., London.

Figure 65.

Figures 65–67. *Gramp,* photographs (1976), Mark Jury and Dan Jury. Narrative text by Mark Jury, Grossman Publishers, A Division of The Viking Press, New York.

nist's excretions, we are told, are a never-ending torment to him—a torment that derives from the uncleanliness, the unseemliness, and the odor, and ultimately from knowing that another person must take part in it.

The photojournal *Gramp* (Figures 64–67, 78, 96, 99, 107, 114) chronicles through camera and diary notation a family's tender caring for a grandfather through senility and death. When Gramp loses bladder and bowel control, Nana, captured in a photograph holding up the soiled, full underpants, voices everyone's feelings as she acknowledges the indignity of the ordeal. Unlike Ivan Ilyich, the *Gramp* series suggests that even a protracted death can be borne with dignity, grace, and great love.

The crisis was so unexpected and the pace so hectic that none of us realized that the intolerable time had undoubtedly arrived. On that day, Nan voiced the feelings of everyone when she said, to no one in particular, ''Gosh it's an awful ordeal.''

Figure 66.   Figure 67.

No matter how loving and caring the family member, the tedium can become unbearable. In "Notes of a Survivor," Robert Anderson describes the strain of continual care of his bed-ridden, dying wife (Figure 68). Worn down from attending to her all-consuming daily needs, he escapes, though not without questioning his intentions. He takes the garbage to the town dump and stays away much longer than usual.

It had been a rough day for me after a series of rough days of preparing meals, tending, cleaning up. It was suppertime and dusk. I took the garbage to the town dump a few miles away and I stayed away much longer than I usually stayed away, almost an hour, driving recklessly through twisting country roads, feeling what?—I don't know. Freedom? Exhilaration? Some death wish?

Figure 68. "Notes of a Survivor." In *The Patient, Death and the Family*. Robert Anderson (1974). Stanley B. Troupe and William A. Green (Eds.), Charles Scribner's & Sons, New York.

The theme of the imprisonment of daily care is similarly expressed in *The Shadow Box*. In a hospice-like cottage, Mark has chosen to stay with his terminally ill lover, Brian, until death. Mark is so exhausted by the demands of the routine that he feels as if he too is being eaten alive by the cancer. Beverly, Brian's ex-wife, comes to visit and Mark explodes (Figure 69).

You can wipe up the mucous and the blood
and the piss and excrement. You can burn
the sheets and boil his clothes, but it's
still there. You can smell it on him.

You can smell it on me. It gets into your
blood . . . you can taste it on him, you can
swallow it and feel it inside your belly like
a sewer.

You wake up at night and you shake and
you spit. You try to vomit it out of you.
Inside every word, every move, every day,
every touch, every night, it lies down with
you and gets in between you. It's sick and
putrid and soft and rotten and it is killing
me.

Figure 69.   *The Shadow Box.* Michael Cristopher. Copyright 1979 by Michael Cristopher.
Reprinted by permission of Samuel French, Inc., New York.

Beverly slaps Mark, and the anger gives way to tears. In broken whispers, Mark admits, "I don't want him to die. I don't please . . . ." They reach out to console each other in their pain.

In *The Shadow Box,* readers and viewers are witnessing "anticipatory" grief work, the emotions of an expected loss and the turmoil that accompanies it. Grief is not a disease. It is a desperate clinging, a refusal to let go. Sorrow is an expected, acceptable response; anger (Figures 70, 71) less so. Yet both are expressions of love and longing. To be bereaved is to be robbed. It feels as if we are being divested and disconnected. We do not let go willingly. Hanging onto the anger is a kind of protective covering in itself—a bulwark against the flood of sadness we fear might overwhelm us.

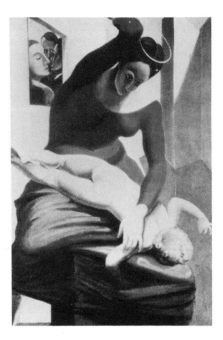

Figure 70. *I Hate You.* Postcard. Copyright 1991 by Rebecca Wilson.

Figure 71. *The Blessed Virgin Chastises Jesus Before Three Witnesses* (1926), Max Ernst. Copyright 1990 Artists Rights Society, Inc., New York/SPADEM, Paris.

Tears unwashed
are stones upon the heart
that choke the healing
stream

Figure 72. Herman Melville. Source unknown.

Unresolved grief, says Colin Murray Parkes (1965), may prove to be as important to psychopathology as inflammation is to pathology. Like a wound kept too tightly bandaged, it will continue to fester. Herman Melville speaks of the healing power of tears that when "unwashed" do "choke the healing stream" (Figure 72). Sorrow, says a Shakespearean character, must be given tongue, because unspoken grief can be injurious (Figure 73). The expression of anger and guilt—in addition to tears—are ways of giving words to sorrow.

> *Give sorrow words.*
> *The grief that does not speak,*
> *whispers the o'erfraught heart*
> *and bids it break.*

Figure 73. *The Tragedy of Macbeth*, Act IV, Scene III. William Shakespeare. In *Shakespeare, Complete Works* (1952). Harcourt Brace and Company, Orlando, FL.

In a Koren cartoon (Figure 74), a monstrous animal looms behind a couple sitting on a couch. A representation of unconscious fear, it is the surfacing and venting of unexpected thoughts and feelings that keep the situation bearable. When fright, rage, and pain are expressed, we are able to find peace.

Humor is another way of uncorking anxiety and distress and achieving relief, albeit temporary. Woody Allen's physician tells him that death is not good for his ulcer. In a child's drawing of two surgeons operating, one drops the heart and the other exclaims, "Oh shit!" (Figure 75). When the adolescent explained his drawing to the class, he revealed that his grandfather had undergone open heart surgery a few weeks earlier. The child managed to deflect the focus of his anxiety for his grandfather and his own sadness onto the physicians. In a class discussion of the drawing, the adolescents blamed the potential death on the incompetence of the physicians much as they blamed the 1986 space shuttle disaster on the incompetence of NASA. The doctors, they decided, were sloppy, inept, and casual.

"We deal with it by talking about it."

Figure 74. Cartoon: "We deal with it by talking about it." Drawing by Edward Koren (1975). The New Yorker Magazine, Inc., New York.

Figure 75. Adolescent's drawing: "Oh Shit!" In Sandra L. Bertman (1979-1980), "The Arts: A Source of Comfort and Insight for Children Who Are Learning About Death." *Omega* 10(2).

Some coping mechanisms are less palatable than others. Jokes circulating in primary and secondary school classrooms just after the shuttle catastrophe focused on the macabre death of the astronauts: "What is the official NASA cereal? Space Crispies"; "What's worse than glass in baby food? Astronauts in tuna." Students vilified the teacher-astronaut as stupid: "Seven months of training and she still went to pieces after takeoff"; "How do you get rid of a teacher? Challenge her" (Simons, 1985). The horror of having the unexpected happen, a beloved teacher so suddenly and violently taken from them, was too close to home. The disguise of such "sick humor" is not as transparent as it seems.

Stephen Spender's couplet (Figure 76) encompasses the self-blame, guilt, and feelings of inadequacy that saddle the survivor. The recriminations and remorse inherent in the "what if's" and "if only's" can be alleviated by the release availed by venting, talking, or respite. The hospice philosophy identifies the family, not the patient, as the unit of care. Relief for the family member is built into the treatment plan. If only hospice care had been available to the protagonist who stole a few extra private moments at the garbage dump.

> *At first you did not love enough;*
> *and afterwards, you love too much.*

Figure 76.   "The Double Shame." Stephen Spender. In *Collected Poems* (1986). Random House, New York.

Yet paradoxically, it seems to be participation itself that is the ultimate balm. In *Last Letter to the Pebble People*, a mother is grateful that she did not protect her daughter from the indignities of her father's disease, that she offered her instead new resources of strength and character that could serve her well in the future (Figures 77, 78).

Several times she helped with the three-person task of cleaning up after a bowel movement. I realize now how we would have cheated her had we succumbed to a false sense of decency. The burden of grief has been easier to bear because we worked so hard. The physical labor of Aldie's care seemed to cleanse us of lingering guilts that so often plague the bereaved.

Figure 77. *Last Letter to the Pebble People.* Virginia H. Hine (1977). St. Alden's in the Weeds, Miami, FL.

Figure 78. *Gramp*, photographs (1976), Mark Jury and Dan Jury. Narrative text by Mark Jury, Grossman Publishers, A Division of The Viking Press, New York.

Theme V
Tolerance for Ambivalence: The Land of the Sick versus the Land of the Well

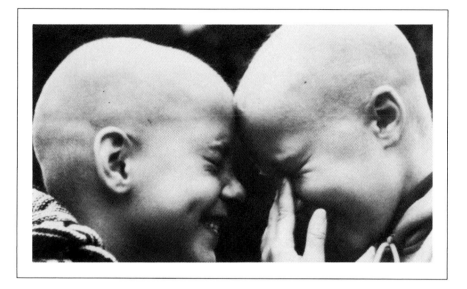

Detail of *Cancer Camp* (See page 72).

. . . stay with me even as I am falling away from you.

Free Fall

Just as a family member needs respite from constant attention to the world of the dying, so the dying relative needs to be free of continual reminders of the world soon to be left behind (Figures 79–82). Withdrawal and disengagement, at times, may be highly adaptive coping mechanisms. Jessamyn West (*The Woman Said Yes*) is surprised and silenced by her sister's wish to avoid hearing about the outside world (Figure 83).

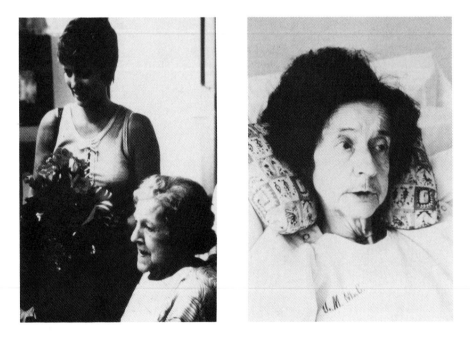

Figure 79.   Figure 80.

Figures 79–82.   University of Massachusetts Medical Center, Palliative Care Service, photographs in Bertman Collection.

Figure 81.

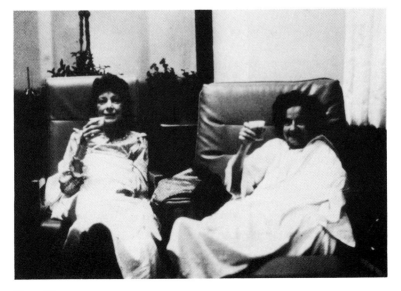

Figure 82.

> I said goodbye to all that last
> summer. It wasn't easy but I did,
> and it's over. All I'm saying
> goodbye to now is pain. You get
> this cannonball in your guts and
> see how much you care about the
> moonlight on the sand dunes.

Figure 83.   Excerpt from *The Woman Said Yes.* Copyright 1976 by Jessamyn West. Reprinted by permission of Harcourt Brace Jovanovich, Inc., Orlando, FL.

One would suppose that playing a favorite piece of music would bring pleasure and peace; however, in *Last Letter to the Pebble People,* it evokes restlessness and agitation. The author/spouse comes to understand how these former worldly loves are now disturbing interruptions, drawing her husband back toward thoughts and feelings associated with this world; a movement he no longer wished to make: "In a life-and-death struggle we always assume that the struggle is for life *against* death. I wonder if there is a time in each human life when life itself becomes the lesser state and the victorious must struggle for death" (Hine, 1977). Stewart Alsop (1973), speaking of himself, has phrased it well: "A dying man needs to die, as a sleepy man needs to sleep, and there comes a time when it is wrong, as well as useless, to resist."

Sometimes nurses, aides, and other patients seem to be able to read and respond to concerns when family members cannot. For Ivan Ilyich, comfort comes from his manservant, Gerasim, who sits with him, supporting Ilyich's legs on his shoulders. The author of *Free Fall* admits of her husband that his presence is too painful a reminder that their trajectories—he toward living, she toward dying—are so diametrically opposed (Figure 84). She finds consolation in what Blanche DuBois, the

His mere presence reminds me that he is a living person and that I am dying, and I become more comfortable when he is gone.

Figure 84.   *Free Fall.* JoAnn Kelley Smith (1975). Used by permission of Judson Press, Valley Forge, PA.

heroine of *A Streetcar Named Desire*, calls "the kindness of strangers" (Williams, 1947). An astute hospital staff member responds to her needs of the moment through presence, prayer, and a slice of pizza:

> Grace is one of these gifted nurses . . . On another occasion she and a friend visited me after working hours just to see how I was doing. I was in good spirits that night so they asked if they could get me something to eat. "What would taste good?" Grace asked. "Pepperoni pizza," I said. And in less than an hour they returned with the best pizza I had ever eaten (Smith, 1975).

In a scene from the play *As Is* (Hoffman, 1985), the patients confess with relief that, at least when they come to the AIDS clinic, they don't have to lie. In *Walking Through the Fire*, Laurel Lee voices this rapport with other cancer patients, adding a tinge of camaraderie (Figure 85).

Greyhound bus drivers honk at each other while passing on the highway. Women with tiny children the same age smile at each other in the supermarkets. The veterans and I had cancer. It put us in the same fraternity.

Figure 85.   *Walking Through the Fire.* Laurel Lee (1974). Journal manuscript, Equinox Collection.

Figures 86 and 87 express this bond visually: the unselfconsciousness of children who have undergone chemotherapy or the bonding that occurs in survivors of open-heart surgery.

Figure 86. *Cancer Camp.* Mary Ellen Mark/Library, New York.

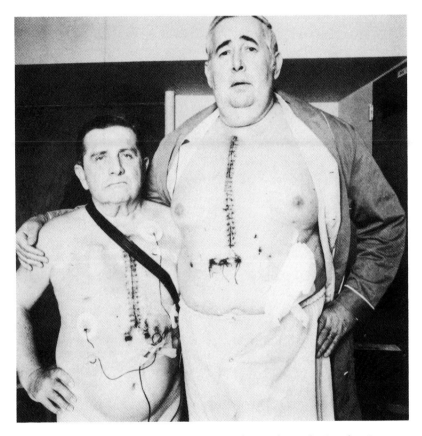

Figure 87. *Patients: The Experience of Illness* (1980), Mark Rosenberg. The Saunders Press, Philadelphia.

Yet accompanying this separation from life and all its painful reminders comes a paradoxical need not to be left alone. This ambivalence is expressed in *Free Fall*:

> I give you up a little bit in my free-fall experience. But at the same time I don't want you to give me up. Maybe that's selfish—maybe this is how a dying person expresses his selfishness—that I want you to stay with me even as I am falling away from you (Smith, 1975).

Ironically, by tending so competently to physical needs, the hospital environment isolates the dying person from the necessary support of human intimacy, crucial at any stage of life and intensified during serious illness. A George Price cartoon brings the point home (Figure 88).

In spite of her protestations about wanting to move away from emotional interactions with her husband, the dying wife in *Free Fall* wants her husband to stay with her overnight in the hospital. She offers a credible argument for double beds and door locks in hospital rooms when she expresses the soothing power of simply sleeping together (Figure 89).

The reassurance of touch is often sought by patient and partner alike. Munch's graphic *Compassion* (Figure 90) was retitled *Consolation* by one patient support group. This group was divided on the question of who is supporting whom? Is the strength coming from the "healthy" partner or from the patient? It doesn't seem to matter. Both need to be in intimate, wordless proximity. An Alice Walker poem epitomizes the healing that takes place through touch, the real medicine of human interaction (Figure 91).

Figure 88.   Cartoon: "Visiting hours are now over, Mrs. Glenhorn." Drawing by George Price (1969). The New Yorker Magazine, Inc., New York.

If your husband or wife could stay with you overnight, the healthy mate could take away a lot of the anxiety and even some of the pain by giving assurances that, "I will be here! I will support you; no matter what happens, you can count on me; we're in this together and I love you."

Figure 89.   *Free Fall.* JoAnn Kelley Smith (1975). Used by permission of Judson Press, Valley Forge, PA.

Figure 90. *Compassion* (1894), Edvard Munch. Drypoint and acquatint, 210 × 213 mm. Nasjonalgalleriet, Oslo, Norway. Photograph by Jacques Lathion, Nasjonalgalleriet.

Grandma sleeps with
my sick
      grand-
pa so she
 can get him
during the night
medicine
to stop
the pain

  In
the morning
  clumsily
   I
wake
  them

Her eyes
look at me
from under-
         neath
his withered
 arm

The
medicine
is all
 in
her long
 un-
    braided
     hair.

Figure 91. "Medicine." Alice Walker. From *Once: Poems* (1968). Copyright 1968 by Alice Walker. Reprinted by permission of Harcourt Brace Jovanovich, Orlando, FL.

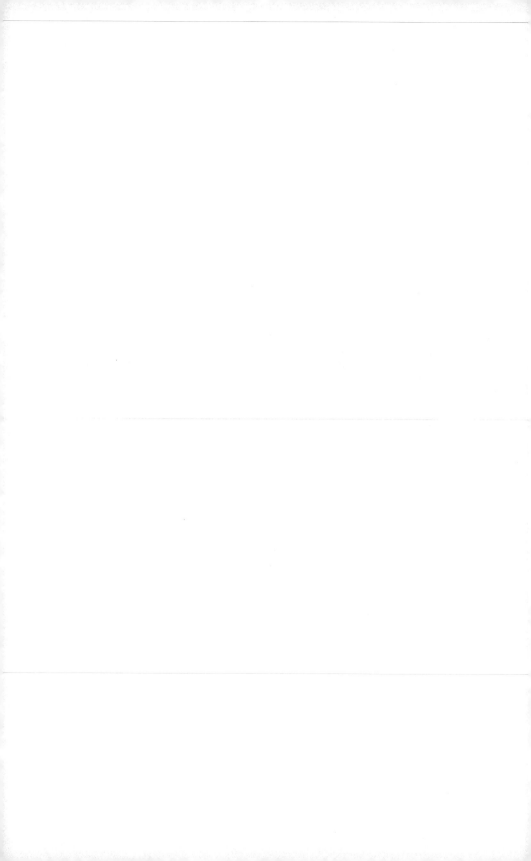

Theme VI
The Moment of Death

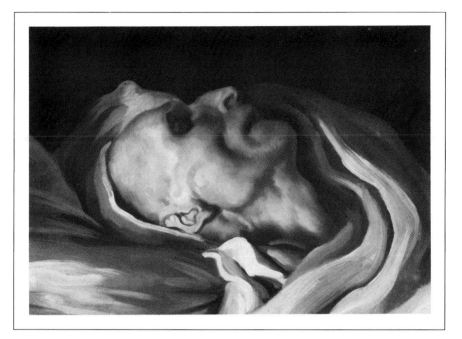

Figure 100.   *After Death, Study of a Severed Head* (1797–1883), Charles Emile Callandre de Champmartin. Oil on canvas, 1818/19, 45.6 × 55.6 cm. A. A. Munger Collection, 1937.502. Copyright 1990 The Art Institute of Chicago. All rights reserved.

In place of death there was light.

The Death of Ivan Ilyich, Tolstoy

No matter how prepared for death we think we are and no matter how anxious we are for its occurrence, the moment of death is an awesome event, capable of eliciting unexpected strong feelings. Edvard Munch portrays this moment in two ways (Figures 92, 95): withdrawn isolation and detached communion. Here again, hospital management

Figure 92. *Death in the Sickroom* (1895), Edvard Munch. Oil on canvas, 150 × 167.5 cm. Nasjonalgalleriet, Oslo, Norway. Photograph by Jacques Lathion, Nasjonalgalleriet.

After having taken care of her every want and need for five years, I was forced out of the room a second after she died by an intern I had never seen before who wanted to be alone while he pronounced her dead.

Figure 93. "Notes of a Survivor." Robert Anderson. In *The Patient, Death and the Family* (1974). Stanley B. Troupe and William A. Green (Eds.). Charles Scribner's and Sons, New York.

Figure 94. *Mourners* (1977), Benny Andrews. 14 × 10. Reprinted in *Between the Lines* (1978). Pella Publishing Company, New York. Courtesy of the artist.

routines are not flexible enough to maximize the possibilities of such moments. In the essay "Notes of a Survivor," the husband who had taken care of his dying wife reacts with appropriate outrage at being forced out of her hospital room at the moment of death (Figure 93). A Benny Andrews illustration (Figure 94) effectively dramatizes these sentiments.

The moment of death sets into motion a sort of life review for all participants in the event. It is a time for insight and forgiveness, the last chance to say the unsaid (Figures 96–98), the optimal moment to inoculate the bereaved against the lingering guilts that so often plague them. If the Dylan Thomas poem "Do Not Go Gentle" (Figure 49) could have a sequel, the dialogue might be expressed in the language of Anatole Broyard's short story, "What the Cystoscope Said," in which the moment of death impels an adult son to voice previously unacknowledged kinship with his father (Figure 97). More than an act of love for the father, the words are surprisingly healing for the son.

"Pop," I said, "You've been a good father, just what I wanted. Just what you were supposed to be. You made me into a good son, and I'll always remember you did what you were supposed to do, and you don't have to reproach yourself for anything. I'm proud of you, and you can be proud of yourself, too. I love you Pop, just like a son loves his father, and as a man, too. God bless you, Pop."

I talked to him like this for a long time crouched close, not because I cared whether anyone else heard, but because I wanted him to hear. As I spoke listening to my own words as though they were the judgment of some third party, I realized with a mild astonishment that they were true.

Figure 97. "What the Cystoscope Said." Anatole Broyard. Courtesy of the author.

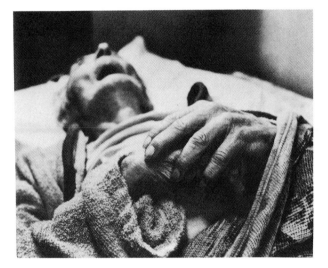

Figure 96. *Gramp*, photographs (1976), Mark Jury and Dan Jury. Narrative text by Mark Jury, Grossman Publishers, A Division of The Viking Press, New York.

One moment can retroactively flood an entire lifetime with meaning. For Ivan Ilyich, who experiences an unresolved, agonized death not unlike the scene portrayed in Beckmann's painting (Figure 10), feeling his son's tears allows him to care, at last, for another human being. Being father and husband for a moment, however brief, enables Ilyich to face death with equanimity (Figure 98). Peace and ease replace terror and pain. In these last moments, Ilyich gives substance to his shallow, unlived life that has become, paradoxically, his death. The powerful expressions captured in Figures 97 and 98 invite speculation about the ecstasy of insight and peace reportedly occurring at the moment of death. (Figures 99 and 100.)

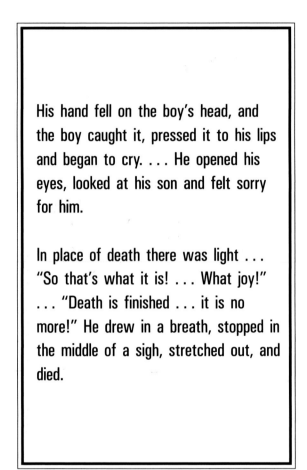

His hand fell on the boy's head, and the boy caught it, pressed it to his lips and began to cry. . . . He opened his eyes, looked at his son and felt sorry for him.

In place of death there was light . . . "So that's what it is! . . . What joy!" . . . "Death is finished . . . it is no more!" He drew in a breath, stopped in the middle of a sigh, stretched out, and died.

Figure 98.   From *The Death of Ivan Ilyich.* Leo Tolstoy (1886). Translated by Rosemary Edmonds (Penguin Classics, 1960). Copyright 1960 by Rosemary Edmonds. Penguin Books, Ltd., London.

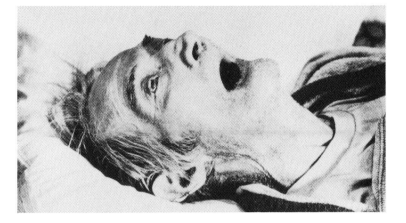

Figure 99. *Gramp*, photographs (1976). Mark Jury and Dan Jury. Narrative text by Mark Jury, Grossman Publishers, A Division of The Viking Press, New York.

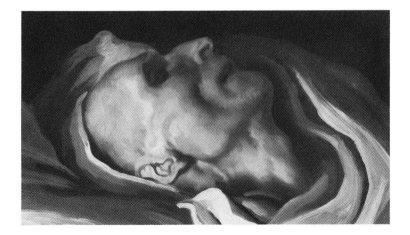

Figure 100. *After Death, Study of a Severed Head* (1797–1883), Charles Emile Callandre de Champmartin. Oil on canvas, 1818/19, 45.6 × 55.6 cm. A. A. Munger Collection, 1937.502. Copyright 1990 The Art Institute of Chicago. All rights reserved.

The intern who forced the husband out of the hospital room (Figure 93) could take a lesson from the gentle behavior of a sensitive nurse who demonstrates in a home situation what he might have done, even in a hospital setting. The nurse not only summons the family to the bedside but also, by gently touching the dead man, gives license to the family to follow suit. She gracefully steps back after the death pronouncement, allowing them to complete their farewells in their own ways. In *Last Letter to the Pebble People*, author Virginia Hine recalls in detail this poignant moment; a moment that will become a painful though precious memory (Figure 101, juxtaposed with Figure 95).

I bent over Aldie to hold him, to press my face next to his, to speak the words I needed to say. I knew he was there, watching from the spaces just above us. But it was the body I had loved so much that I needed to hold and speak to. Then I straightened up and Jennifer embraced him whispering her words of love. She stepped away to make room for Connie, and one by one each person moved to the head of the bed opposite me and held him or touched his hand and spoke as they felt moved.

Figure 101. *Last Letter to the Pebble People.* Virginia H. Hine (1977). St. Alden's in the Weeds, Miami, FL.

Figure 95. *Todesangst (Death Agony)* (1896), Edvard Munch. Lithograph. Graphische Samlung Albertina, Vienna.

Figure 106. *Old Woman Resting Against Old Man* (1915–1936), Gustav Viegland. Granite. Viegland Park, Oslo, Norway.

You cannot prevent the birds of sorrow from flying overhead,
But you can prevent them from building nests in your hair.

Chinese Proverb

Munch's mother at the bedside of *The Dying Child* (Figure 102) or Mary at the bedside of the dead Christ in Mantegna's painting, *The Dead Christ* (Figure 103), are cameos of caring in which union and communion—that is, love—not only ease but also somehow transcend the sting of parting. For example, any revulsion from disfigurement is "kissed" away in Picasso's cubist painting, *The Kiss* (Figure 104). Photographic and sculptural variations on this theme include Figures 103, 105, 106, and 107. In the Ingmar Bergman film, *Cries and Whispers*, the graphic details of the vulgarities of illness—the sweat, vomiting, emaciation, raw pain—recede when Anna, the maid, cradles the dying Agnes in her arms (Figure 108). Bergman evokes a Pieta-like pose of serenity in his characters.

Similar moments are also documented in photographs of touching, real-life instances in several patients' final days: a daughter caring for her mother (Figure 109); a wedding on the University of Massachusetts Palliative Care Unit a few weeks before the bride's death (Figures 110, 111); four generations at the bedside of a family member just a few hours before his death (Figures 112, 113). Perhaps the most evocative juxtaposition is the circularity of life suggested in two photographs of a grandfather holding his baby grandson and, years later, that grandson cradling his dying grandfather (Figures 114, 64). Gerda Lerner, writing of her husband's death in *A Death of One's Own* (Figure 115), epitomizes the crucial role we can play at such a time.

Death, then, not only evokes horror, exhaustion, and separation; it can also be an opportunity for existential communion. It can remind us of the preciousness and wonder of life and of the specialness and connectedness we share with one another. Death is the backdrop against which we play out our mortality and enact our humanity.

To restate the Chinese proverb, the arts cannot stay the flights of the birds of sorrow, they can, perhaps, help us better endure them.

Figure 102.   *The Dying Child* (1885–1886), Edvard Munch. Oil on canvas, 119.5 × 118.5 cm. Nasjonalgalleriet, Oslo, Norway. Photograph by Jacques Lathion, Nasjonalgalleriet. Munch's sister, Sophie, died of tuberculosis at age 15, when the artist was 14. He did several versions of this theme.

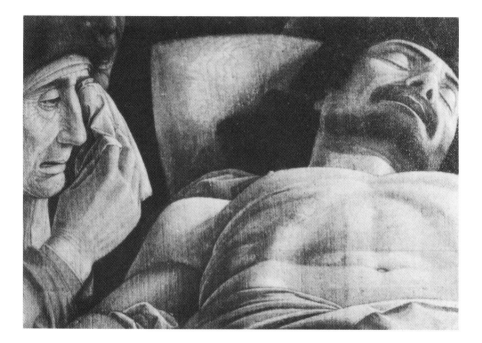

Figure 103. *The Dead Christ* (c. 1460), Andrea Mantegna. Canvas. Grera Gallery, Milan. In Giuseppi Fiocco, *Paintings by Mantegna,* Harry Abrams, Inc., New York.

Figure 104. *Le Baiser (The Kiss)* (1969), Pablo Picasso. Oil on canvas. Copyright 1990 Artists Rights Society, Inc., New York/SPADEM, Paris.

Figure 105. Detail from photograph of Pat and Ron, *Epitaphs For the Living: Words and Images in the Time of AIDS* (1989). Photographs by Billy Howard. Southern Methodist University Press, Dallas.

Figure 106. *Old Woman Resting Against Old Man* (1915–1936), Gustav Viegland. Granite. Viegland Park, Oslo, Norway.

Figure 108. Still photo from *Cries and Whispers* (1972), Ingmar Bergman.

Figure 107. *Gramp*, photographs (1976), Mark Jury and Dan Jury. Narrative text by Mark Jury, Grossman Publishers, A Division of The Viking Press, New York.

Figure 109.   Anna Kaufman Moon. Courtesy of the photographer.

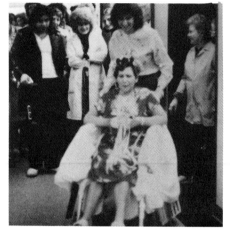

Figure 110.

Figure 111.

Figure 112.

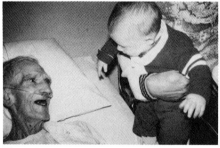

Figure 113.

Figures 110–113.   Photographs, University of Massachusetts Medical Center, Palliative Care
Service, Bertman Collection.

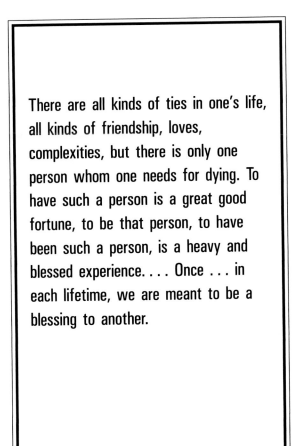

There are all kinds of ties in one's life, all kinds of friendship, loves, complexities, but there is only one person whom one needs for dying. To have such a person is a great good fortune, to be that person, to have been such a person, is a heavy and blessed experience. . . . Once . . . in each lifetime, we are meant to be a blessing to another.

Figure 115.   From *A Death of One's Own*. Gerda Lerner (1978). Reprinted by permission of Gerda Lerner.

Frank Tugend and his grandson, Dan Jury, 1954.

Figure 114. *Gramp*, photographs (1976), Mark Jury and Dan Jury. Narrative text by Mark Jury, Grossman Publishers, A Division of The Viking Press, New York.

Dan Jury and his grandfather, Frank Tugend, 1974.

Figure 64.   *Gramp*, photographs (1976), Mark Jury and Dan Jury. Narrative text by Mark Jury, Grossman Publishers, A Division of The Viking Press, New York.

NOTES

1. See variations on this iconography of death and the *danse macabre* in Ingmar Bergman's film, *The Seventh Seal*, and Woody Allen's one-act play, *Death Knocks*, in *Getting Even*. Allen parodies the traditionally dark-garbed figure by casting him as an awkward "schlep" who on arrival and while "shaking like a leaf" trips over the windowsill and falls into the room.

2. "Middle knowledge," a state of seeming denial, is an inner realization of the gap between what is inferred and what is known about one's terminal condition. See Weisman, A. (1972). *On dying and denying: A psychiatric study of terminality.* New York: Behavioral Publications.

3. Allusion to Dickinson, E. (1979). After great pain a formal feeling comes— [1862]. T. Johnson (Ed.), *The poems of Emily Dickinson* (p. 341). Cambridge, MA: Harvard University Press.

REFERENCES

Allen, W. (1971a). Loser take all. In *Getting even* (p. 20). New York: Random House.

Allen, W. (1971b). Without feathers. In *Getting even* (p. 10). New York: Random House.

Alsop, S. (1973). *Stay of execution.* Philadelphia: Lippincott.

Bernstein, L. (1918). Somewhere. *West side story* [Musical]. Based on a conception of Jerome Robbins. Book by Arthur Laurents. Lyrics by Stephan Sondheim. Columbia Records, OL5230.

Diamant, A. (1990, June 3). AIDS and comfort. *The Boston Globe Magazine.*

Dickinson, E. (1979). My life closed twice before its close—(no. 1732) [1896]. In T. Johnson (Ed.), *The poems of Emily Dickinson* (p. 1166). Cambridge, MA: Harvard University Press.

Freud, S. (1963). P. Riess (Ed.), *General psychological theory* (pp. 104–150). New York: Collier McMillan Books. (See discussion of the unconscious and repression.)

Hine, V. (1977). *Last letter to the pebble people* (p. 115). Miami, FL: St. Alden's in the Weeds.

Hoffman, W. M. (1985). *As is.* New York: Vintage.

Holme, B. (Ed.). (1979). Pyramus and Thisbe. In *Bulfinch's mythology, the Greek and Roman fables illustrated* (pp. 47–48). New York: The Viking Press.

Klee, P. (1933). St. Francis. 5³/4 × 12¹/2. Collection Frau Marietta Preleuthner, Vienna, Austria.

Lifton, R. J. (1961). *History and human survival* (pp. 174–175). New York: Random House.

Mars-Jones, A. (1988). Slim. In E. White & A. Mars-Jones, *The darker proof stories from a crisis* (p. 7). New York: New American Library.

Mars-Jones, A. Op. cit., p. 2.

Maze, E. (1990, June). Scandinavian notebook. In *Scanorama.*

Morganthal, H. J. (1961). Death in the nuclear age. *Commentary* 32, 231–234. (See also Herman Feifel's provocative interpretation of this "sociologic immortality" in the chapter, "Death." (1963). In N. L. Farberow (Ed.), *Taboo topics* (pp. 8–21). New York: Atherton Press, a Division of Prentice-Hall, Inc.

Parkes, C. M. (1965). The clinical study of bereavement in psychiatric patients. *British Journal of Medical Psychology* 38, 25–26.

Rogers, R., & Hammerstein, O. (1943). Poor Jud is dead. *Oklahoma* [Musical]. Original motion picture soundtrack, Capitol Records, Inc., SWA02–595.

Shakespeare, W. (1949). *Romeo and Juliet.* (1595). In R. Gittings (Ed.), *The living Shakespeare* (p. 357). New York: Macmillan.

Siegel, B. (1986). *Love, medicine and miracles.* New York: Harper & Row.

Simons, E. R. (1985, October). The NASA joke cycle: The astronauts and the teacher. *Western folklore* (pp. 261–277). Glendale, CA: California Folklore Society Group.

Smith, J. K. (1975). *Free fall* (pp. 38, 107). Valley Forge, PA: Judson Press.

Sontag, S. (1977). *Illness as metaphor* (pp. 47–49). New York: Farrar, Straus and Giroux.

Tagore, R. (1937). *Collected poems and plays of Rabindranath Tagore.* New York: Macmillan.

Walker, A. (1968). Exercises on themes from life. In *Once: Poems* (pp. 79–81). New York: Harcourt Brace Jovanovich.

Weisman, A. (1970). Psychosocial considerations in terminal care. In B. Schoenberg, A. Carr, D. Peretz, A. Kutscher (Eds.), *Loss and grief: Psychological management in medical practice.* New York: Columbia University Press.

Williams, T. (1980). *A streetcar named desire* [1947] (p. 178). New York: New Directions.

3
Responses to the Images

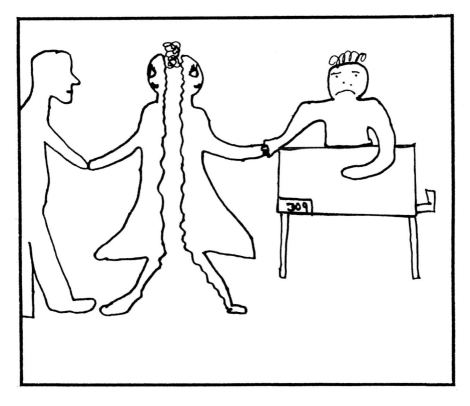

An oncology nurse displays literally the painful division of allegiance that occurs at the hands of her patient and family members, friends, doctors, and hospital policy or medical staff.

Figure 116. Image from nurse, University of Massachusetts Medical Center, 1990.

Chapter 3

Responses to the Images

Zorba:	*Why do the young die? Why does anybody die? Tell me. What's the use of all your damn books if they can't answer questions like that? What the hell can they do for you?*
Scholar:	*Well, they tell me about the agony of the man who can't answer questions like yours.[1]*

This chapter demonstrates how five specific populations have reacted to the issues of facing death in the context of terminal illness. The responses of these audiences make clear the value of the arts as evocative tools for people of all ages and professions. Participants ranged in age from 13 years old to mature adults and in profession from lay volunteers from a variety of occupations to experienced health professionals. The groups include

Junior and senior high school students (West Virginia)
College students (Lesley College, Cambridge, MA)
Medical students (University of Massachusetts Medical School, Worcester, MA)
Graduate nurses (University of Massachusetts School of Nursing, Boston, MA)
Hospice volunteers (State-Wide Conference, MA)

All group members filled out a Death Attitude Questionnaire and addressed the question of a most memorable image from the double-slide lecture presentation (see Appendixes 1 and 2). Members of three groups were asked to come to the viewing having drawn or devised their own personal image of death. Permission has been granted from members of each group for use of their comments, sketches, and suggestions.

RESPONSES OF JUNIOR AND SENIOR HIGH SCHOOL STUDENTS (SCIENCE AWARD FINALISTS), WEST VIRGINIA

The junior and senior high school population consisted of 57 students from across West Virginia competing at a National Science Symposium sponsored by the United States Army Research Office. Each student was the finalist from his or her respective school. Students ranged in age from 13 to 17 years old.

Students were asked to complete the Death Attitude Questionnaire before the double-slide presentation and to comment on a "most memorable image" after the presentation. Students were first alerted to the strong nature of the material and then invited to reflect on the type of death they would choose for themselves, given the option of a sudden death and a lingering terminal illness. Sudden death was the choice of all but one student, who explained that because death would be so final, she wanted to "hang on" as long as possible. The ideal scenario, the group agreed—if one *must* have a death scene—would be outdoors, most likely alone or, if indoors, in one's sleep, surrounded by family, friends, and (especially) pets and while listening to a "Walkman."

Twenty-four of the 33 students completed the most memorable image exercise. The images chosen included literal and symbolic depictions of the afterlife or immortality, *Death of Socrates*, Cummings's poem "dying is fine," cartoons, and artifacts from popular culture, photographs from *Gramp*, and snapshots of patients on the University of Massachusetts Palliative Care Unit.

Two girls chose the anatomical gift (Figure 41), one because it was "comforting."

One student saw no such noble or redeeming factor about death at all. She chose the Cummings poem (Figure 15) because "the thought of dying is, at least, still the thought of life, whereas death is definite and unchangeable." She believed that one is still actively involved and very much alive as long as one is thinking.

Two 13-year-old girls chose *The Death of Socrates* (Figure 5). One girl found it reassuring and comforting because death did not appear to be the literal end. She saw this painting as a reminder that one is moving on "a new beginning" (extrapolating this from the figure's finger pointing heavenward). The other girl commented that everyone cared enough to be there at the time of Socrates' death, and she added the hope that her friends and family would care enough to be present when she dies.

Depictions of the new beginning or afterlife were chosen by other students. Without naming the 15th century woodcut, *The Goodman on his Deathbed* (Figure 6), or El Greco's *Burial of Count Orgaz* (Figure 25), one student described the "little heaven full of caring people" prominent in both as most memorable. She wanted to know that she would be welcome in heaven and that this would be the destiny in store for her. Another chose *The Goodman on his Deathbed* because it felt "appropriate."

Eight students chose pop-culture images. The sardonic get-well cards and the cartoons were appreciated for their humor. Two youngsters commented on the get-well card, "We all hate to see you sick . . . So none of us are coming to see you" (Figure 50). The humor was interpreted as the "sometimes truthful way that people feel." "Too bad you're sick but . . . ." (Figure 53) was another popular choice because students perceived an inherent truth to the concept. Consequently, another animated discussion centered around the theme of the victim as blameworthy, and then the connotations of the word "victim" itself.

Three boys chose the cartoon of dinosaurs smoking (Figure 56)—one because of the humor and his familiarity with Larson's comic strip, "The Far Side," and two because they were strongly against smoking. One student, who felt the cartoon might help someone quit smoking, thought the presentation made fun of death, and "death isn't funny." Another wrote that the smoking dinosaurs showed how absentminded and careless people are when they smoke. One student added "the fact [is] my dad smokes and shortens his lifespan."

Two students chose the cartoon of the elderly couple sitting in the hospital bed (Figure 87). Though they found it humorous, they also found it true; it made them laugh; and "it shows older people can still have spunk."

One boy chose what he defined as "sick humor," the *Oh Shit!* illustration (Figure 75), which elicited a sensitive recollection:

> When the Challenger disaster occurred, I was sick at home from school. I have followed faithfully the U.S. Space Program since age 2, and seeing this happen live on television was like watching a brother die. The news, CBS, ABC, NBC, all of them relentlessly showed this tragedy over and over. I locked myself in my room until my mom returned home. This was one of the worst experiences of my life.
>
> Upon returning to my school, I was bombarded by "humor" in its sickest form. The "Need Another Seven Astronauts" joke pissed me off to no end. Maybe the person who told me this was not aware of my grief, but this kind of 'humor' . . . I just don't know.

The photographs of grandchildren and great-grandchildren at the deathbed (Figures 107, 112, 113) were chosen for emotional reasons by two girls, both of whom were saddened or depressed by them. Though one appreciated the need to learn about death, she wished "it wasn't so depressing." The closeup of the baby and the dying man (Figure 11) "upset" the other student. "It is sad when people die, but if they are sick at least they are put out of their misery," she added.

One student chose as most memorable the entire presentation. She found it consoling and appreciated how it made her think. She referred to "a lot of close friends . . . five to be exact . . . who were killed within a year. Seeing those photographs made me think of my grief when my friends and grandparents died. In a way I now feel a sort of relief, but then I felt alone and very sad because I was so close to my friends and grandparents, because I loved and still do love and miss them very much."

Five students mentioned images from *Gramp* (Figures 64, 96, 107, 114), one because her own grandmother was terminally ill with cancer. Another was upset by the photograph of the girl sitting with her dying grandfather (Figure 105) "obviously to say goodbye, it was really sad." Identifying herself as the type of person who hardly ever cries, she explained further, "It was a situation where you have to say goodbye to someone, knowing you'll never see him again, and if you really care about the person, it's really hard to let go. The presentation helped me understand the whole concept of death better. It let me see different points of view instead of just my own." Two students commented on the juxtaposition of the grandfather carrying grandson/grandson carrying grandfather (Figures 114, 64). One was simply touched "because the man had helped the grandson throughout his life and now it was his turn to help"; the other because "It shows how fragile life is and how quickly it can pass you by."

When conducting such a presentation, the group leader should be aware that some participants will have difficulty with the upsetting nature of this subject matter. Responses from these students can range from flippant remarks to anger to absolute silence. Participants may be either emotionally unprepared to confront their own mortality or have suffered a loss—recently or in the past—too painful to revive at the time of the presentation. To attempt to assist them to release some of their self-imposed restraints in a one- or two-session class can be damaging and may cause further pain. The most positive action the group leader can take is to alert the class ahead of time of the nature and power of the material, of the voluntary aspect of their participation, and of the availability of resources—including himself or herself—for private consultation.

Regardless of the prevalent misconception that we can spare our children the pain of personal tragedy, the responses of these adolescents indicate quite clearly that they have thought about aging and death long enough to have developed informed opinions about these issues. Although pop-culture images generally evoke the most enthusiastic reaction from younger audiences, there was, nevertheless, sufficient response to the more classical images, which indicates the universal appeal of great art, irrespective of age or experience.

RESPONSES OF GRADUATE STUDENTS, LESLEY COLLEGE, CAMBRIDGE, MA

Approximately 2 weeks before the seminar began, a class of creative arts graduate students in education at Lesley College in Cambridge, MA was asked to complete the Death Attitude Questionnaire and to create a picture or image related to their concerns about or attitude toward death. They were told that the scene could be based on real or imagined experience. On an attached sheet of paper, they were invited to explain their drawings and the reasons they chose to depict "Facing Death" as they did.

The images that resulted were compelling, colorful, and symbolic. The media used included pencil, ball point pen, colored markers, pastels, crayon, and watercolor. Some drawings depicted personal anxieties and danger. In Figure 117 a black-crayoned plane is flown by a black-garbed, blindfolded figure in a sky covered with black clouds. It was accompanied by the explanation that the artist was "being scared because there is no rescue." Figure 118 depicts the fear of death meta-

Figure 117.

Figure 118.

phorically as the ominous presence of a black snakelife figure coiling through multicolored plains "always around, sometimes visible and sometimes not, but always in the garden called life."

Figure 119.

In Figure 119, animals, water, and spiky lines are used to portray the sense of danger associated with death. An opened-mouthed shark peers over a wave in a large sea, at the floor of which are same jagged abstractions, possibly primordial forms. In the upper corner of this drawing is a flying bird with something in its beak. The images are described as "scavengers that hunt, claw, screech, and peck and wait and then come for the dead." The birds are viewed also as "symbols of transformation with the ability to fly." Though water instills fear, it also allows the body and spirit to float. According to this student, even the expansiveness of the sea, which occupies most of the space on the paper, is to be viewed as the entire cycle of life and death, the known and unknown, ". . . infinite possibility impossible for humans to master." The student describes the sea's ability to inspire her with feelings of calm, violence, exhilaration, fear, freedom, and peace. Water is often symbolic of the unconscious, or the journey, the terrain between life and death. Consider its use in baptism, by Dante, and in the classical image in Greek mythology of Charon, death's boatman, ferrying dead souls across the river Styx from the shore of life to Hades.

Figure 120 stresses this bipolar point of view. The association of death with the dark is seen as part of the yin-yang, day-night duality of life. Castaneda's *Don Juan* ("Let Death Be Your Companion") was quoted. Realizing that fear is instructive and is therefore a pathway to growth, the student expresses a desire to become familiar with it. He attempts to know death better by drawing three figures that represent different aspects of himself and his bipolar attitude toward death: his shadow, skeletal death, leaps from the earth in abandon; his angel, playful, attends; his guide, seated comfortably in a Buddha position and playing a stringed instrument, is present. A tombstone, sun, and moon frame the composition.

Figure 120.

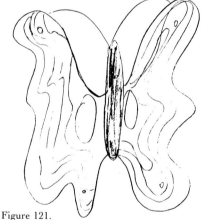

Figure 121.

Some students envisioned death as a transition to a higher spiritual development. A butterfly (Figure 121) symbolized death perfectly for one who felt that while we are in our bodies, we are actually "in the darkness" and that shedding the physical self represents moving into the light or "going home." For another student a beautiful bird (Figure 122) peacefully merges into a backdrop of colors. She explained that her drawing represents "a wistful hope for recognized and conscious transition of being or reality." The bird reminded her of a childhood story about a crane maiden coming to terms peacefully with physical death. The theme of death "opening" into a higher level of awareness is handled by another

Figure 122.

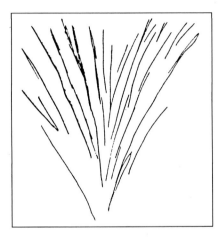

Figure 123.

student as an abstract explosive eruption of "yellow, light that is also deeper," and midnight blue, which is "more real" (Figure 123).

One student's main concern was dying young. His picture (Figure 124)—a cone, point-side down—represents the exfoliation of his life with the passage of the years. The year 1977 is inscribed near the bottom of the cone; farther up, 1987. "Year after year I become more alive," he wrote. "I learn more and am able to do more." Broken lines representing death periodically pierce the inverted funnel. These lines begin to appear above 1987. "I hope they don't make their appearance until around the year 2040. By then I should be ready to die," he writes.

Because the images that come to mind for one student were "too definite and specific," she created an abstract drawing (Figure 125), intended to symbolize the intense emotions surrounding other peoples' or animals' deaths and how they affected her. She adds that her image might also apply to feelings about her own death. The colors are dark, the composition unsettling—the whole signifying "different levels and changes of loneliness, despair, longing, sadness, anger, confusion."

Another said death would be "a long dark end . . . nothing really going on after it happened. Everything is just so dark and it's never over." A motionless corpse and disembodied faces outlined in green are visible through a wash of black watercolor (Figure 126). The explanation betrays concerns of emotional distancing and physically "being forgotten . . . people go on without me (they should, but that's scary) . . . not existing anymore . . . fading into nothingness . . . darkness."

Two images focus specifically on the Christian concept of afterlife. Figure 127 marks the transition to eternal existence with God. The student cited the Biblical text, *John 3:16*, in her explanation: "not something to be feared but embraced with faith and thanksgiving." Figure 128 is an animated drawing, a smiling "welcoming committee" of two, Jesus and Angel Gabriel: "I have to think of death with the Lord and angels and happiness, or I couldn't go on. Plus, I am Catholic and I believe things will be fine."

Several students dealt explicitly with the theme of separation and grief. One used "simplistic" figures to render her view (Figure 129), since she felt "quite innocent and simple" about her death. She depicts a featureless individual who has just died caught between the two halves of a broken heart. On the left, with facial expressions of sadness, the survivors reach out to the deceased, "holding on." The student assumed death is hardest for them. On the right, smiling individuals also reach out to the deceased. In accordance with her religious beliefs, she saw herself reunited with those who have gone before her: "They now have the more

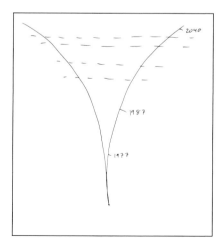

Figure 124.

Figure 125.

Figure 126.

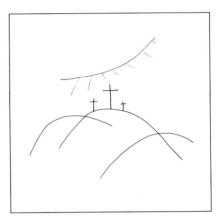

Figure 127.

Figure 128.

Figure 129.

Figure 130.

positive hold." Lurking behind this comforting thought, however, is a series of question marks acknowledging fear of the unknown. There are four holding-on figures, five welcoming figures, and seven question marks.

One student drew her own funeral and afterlife (Figure 130). Her body lies surrounded by loved ones who "are grieved in the parting as I grieve in the leaving," while she is received by angels and her grandfather, being led through a "tunnel" to the next reality.

Another student to whom the most threatening aspect of death is the severance of human connection showed a black figure holding on to its own bleeding umbilical cord attached to its heart (Figure 131): "My heart and its life-line that connects one to all those I love will now be cut." The black figure, surrounded by a yellow glow, symbolic of the world of Spirit and pure God, stands under an archway, apart from the colorful world of life. The figure is black, "black as the Unknown within me, black as my unknown Death, black for oblivion." She believed her body will be forgotten in the minds of the living. She found these thoughts painful, "hence the drops and pool of blood." She speculated that the pain, as well as her view of death (anything but a gentle parting no matter how it might occur in her life's end), derives from the pain of her brother's death.

Three other images depicted personal recollections associated with family members. Figure 132 represents a grandmother the way she was remembered a month before her death. Figure 133 relates to a dream about a father who had faced surgery several years before for a brain

Figure 131.

tumor. Figure 134 conveys the effect of a brother-in-law's death. In the first drawing, the realistic treatment of the grandmother, expressionless and alone in a hospital bed with side rails raised, is not softened by colored sheets and bright plastic flowers, symbols interpreted as the hospital's attempt at cheerfulness. Quite the contrary, the student wrote, "She was left to slide into the cold side railing on the bed, and the nurses were completely impersonal . . . . I don't believe that plastic flowers help, no matter how nice they may look." Apparently quite ready to die, her grandmother's refusal to wear glasses, use her hearing aid or eat is interpreted as a death wish. On the occasion of the visit, this aged woman became animated and connected. "When she saw me, she talked quite a lot and could understand what I said (when she could hear it) and held my hand with an incredible grip . . . ." The granddaughter could identify with the symbolic giving up: "That was the first time I really thought that her thinking might not be on a different level from what mine would be in her situation, even though she was 94 . . . She was just as afraid of dying—gripping my hand to hold on the same way I would hold onto someone (at 24) if I were going to die."

Figure 132.

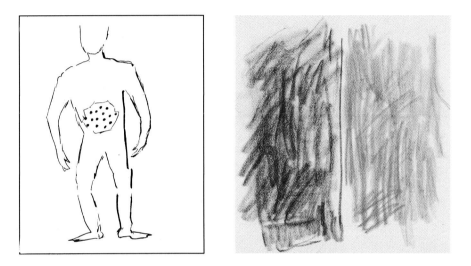

Figure 133.   Figure 134.

The student who dreamed of her father wrote that fears about the possibility of his death was suggestive of her own mortality. Her image (Figure 133) "of being able to see inside myself and see many small blue tumors growing there," admittedly "very frightening to me at the time," is the outline of a figure in the center of which is a circle containing a series of blue dots. The choice of blue to represent cancer—the color for healing and peace—and the fact that the blue dots are encapsulated, is hopeful, suggestive of the anticipated positive outcome.

An image relating to a brother-in-law's death (Figure 134) is also portrayed through color, a composition of two equal abstract blocks—one black, one yellow. After her brother-in-law's death, everything in this student's daily life seemed muddled and bleak. She noted that she was gradually able to enjoy life again "without feeling guilty." She explained how her thoughts eventually turned from black ("full of doubt") to hope, lightness, and life. "I guess Jim's death seemed black, like a bottomless pit—not knowing where he was now; my own loneliness for him. Then as things became brighter again I 'felt' his presence around me."

• • •

In preparation for the montage of images and commentary, class members were alerted to the strong nature of the material. First they were asked to choose either a sudden death or a lingering terminal illness, and then to share the reasons for their choice. The overwhelming majority (all but 3 of 19) chose sudden death and expressed a desire both to spare themselves physical pain and mental anxiety and to protect their families from emotional suffering.

The group members were next invited to design in words their own ideal death scenarios. Where did they want the event to occur? Whom did they want in attendance? The responses were varied. No one wanted to die in a hospital. Several wanted to be outdoors at the ocean or in the mountains. The majority wanted death to be quick and clean, preferably during sleep. Alternatively, a death surrounded by family and special people—and in one case, a dog—would have been preferable.

The hour-long, double-slide presentation of images described in Chapter 2 followed. Before the discussion, the group was asked to comment briefly in writing on one image relating to their own and/or to choose a memorable image that affected them positively or negatively.

Some surprising relationships between the students' images and those presented from the literary and visual arts became evident. For example, because both are really about "the end . . . the *big* question mark," the black-crayoned plane flown by a blindfolded figure in a black-clouded sky (Figure 117) was compared to the close-up juxtaposition of the dead old man's face (Figure 99) and the death-mask-like portrait (Figure 100). The discussion also included speculation about the importance of the deathbed for gaining insight into the person dying, and for exploring the possibilities of a spiritual state, an all-knowing, accepting afterlife, which many dying persons seem to experience in their final moments.

The student who wanted to embrace death and who saw in this act of acceptance the pathway to growth and understanding, chose the Durer woodcut, *Death and the Soldier* (Figure 20). For him, the death-life duality was captured by the idea of a conversation between the skeleton and figure.

For another student the posture of composure in the face of death (Figure 122) created another interesting juxtaposition: the story of the crane maiden with *The Death of Socrates* (Figure 5). She explained, "As the crane plucks out its own feathers, weaving them into the eternal fabric of the cosmos, so Socrates drinks of the hemlock, rationally and consciously, deliberately choosing to transpose himself out of life and into another reality."

Students saw their works reflected in afterlife depictions. The butterfly (Figure 121) was likened to the fate of Picasso's friend in *Evocation, The Burial of Casagemas* (Figure 31). Another student noted several images depicting death in a religious context. Citing the symbolism of the cross, which signifies the afterlife in her own composition (Figure 127), she commented on its use especially in the 15th-century woodcut, *The Goodman on his Deathbed* (Figure 6). The discussion thus expanded the "afterlife welcoming committee" to include Mary, Peter, and other saints receiving the soul in El Greco's *Burial of Count Orgaz* (Figure 25).

The vagueness of Klimpt's *Spectre of Death* (Figure 42) was chosen as a companion piece to Figure 125, a dark, abstract composition symbolizing longing, sadness, and confusion. These intense emotions were projected onto the group huddled together on one side of Klimpt's decorative composition, and onto the skull and the dark death figure on the other.

The student who sketched the figure caught in the middle of the broken heart (Figure 129) chose Munch's *Death Agony* (Figure 95). She saw her image of separation from loved ones and the grief experienced in this pen and ink sketch—"a person lying in bed close to a group of people and a crowd of people in the distance." The student's figure is featureless: Munch's dying individual lies in the bed, her back to the viewer. The people in the student's drawing are visibly tearful, reaching out to and gazing only at the newly dead figure. The people in Munch's graphic are expressionless, equally isolated from one another. In the student's image the dead have calm, relaxed faces, and, according to her religious beliefs, "the more positive hold." In Munch's graphic, the "dead" are barely visible, only slightly defined. Both works ultimately focus the *viewer's* attention on the survivors; the assumption is that death is hardest for them and accordingly, for the artists who created each work. (*Death Agony* was one of a series of works Munch painted on the death of his sister, Sophie. As in *Death in the Sickroom*, and even *At the Deathbed*, we are witnessing Munch's reminiscences, himself—present or absent—of the family members' personal anguishes. The number of paintings on this theme underscores the artist's attention to his grief.)

The student whose protagonist grasps her own bleeding umbilical cord empathized with the pain of the husband who was told to leave his wife's deathbed (Figure 93). "That is the bleeding heart in my picture, since, to me, death is like that" she wrote. "The least you can have is a few moments with the body of your loved one."

Some choices were predictable. The student who saw death as "completely brown" chose the Wyeth's painting/Burroughs quotation juxtaposition (Figures 39, 40), which to her was expressive of peaceful merging with the earth and natural regeneration. In her words, the juxtaposition represented "an eternal rest, yet continuing to give life as part of nature, earth, soil . . . ."

The student who sketched her grandmother in a nursing home bed (Figure 132) had had a good deal of experience in caring for the elderly. She reported that it was often difficult to care for her clients, even though they were not related to her. She especially disliked bathing or cleaning up after them because she felt these acts were degrading for them. She speculated that some of them would prefer not to be bathed. The embarrassment that often accompanies the loss of autonomy, especially in matters relating to dressing and toileting (particularly explicit in some of the photographs from *Gramps* [Figures 65, 66]) made this student realize the connection between her work at Elder Services and her grandmother's death: ". . . It was extremely hard for me to see her physical deterioration the way I saw the others—because I did not want to see her that way."

One student neither completed the pre-image assignment nor choose an image for discussion. She explained: "I think I really don't want to think about it. It really scared me. Death for me is one big black thing, and I think I try to run away from it. The images made me think about the aspects of death, and because I didn't want to think about it, I couldn't get into it."

The class then commented on other provocative images unrelated to their own pictures. One member of the class chose two images, David's *The Death of Socrates* (Figure 5) and Beckmann's *Large Death Scene* (Figure 10); the former, he explained, because "as a man in our society I feel I should be able to take responsibility for my own death"; the latter, because it graphically demonstrates horror and anguish, "almost madness that the grievers will go through." He saw Beckmann's work in a different light: "the *shadow* [his italics] of the Socrates picture," and he stated he wished to come to terms with both the darks and lights in the face of death.

Two students chose the Wyeth painting (Figure 39) in which the figure merges into the landscape in both color and line. One selected it because of its affinity to her own images of her idealized death—"the flowing into another stage of growth like the preparation of soil to plant a seed; a gentle gradual joining, a feeling of cycle" (Figure 123). The other chose the Wyeth because it offered help with her previously expressed concerns about death. She had symbolized the intense emotions of despair, sadness, anger, and confusion in a harsh, abstract way, and was comforted by the interpretation of the Wyeth as a peaceful, comforting, and nurturing vision of death (Figure 127).

The student who sensed the omnipresence of death "like a shaky animal" (Figure 120) identified with some of the quotations from *Last Letter to the Pebble People* (Figures 77, 101) because her family took care of her father, who had died from cancer a few years earlier. She also cited a *Gramp* juxtaposition, (Figures 114, 64), because it reminded her of the circle of life: "First you're taken care of, then you take care, then you're taken care of again."

The student whose main concern was "not dying young" (Figure 124) found the Gerda Lerner quotation (Figure 115) memorable. It reminded him of precious hours spent with a friend who had died of cancer a few years earlier. He wrote, ["this was] an important experience for both of us. Things came out that would not have, under any other situation."

Moved by the *Free Fall* quotation, which describes sharing a bed together even when the spouse is dying (Figure 89), a student reflected that she had missed out on closeness with her brother in the many years of her childhood, and that just as they started to get close, he died. She acknowledged how alone she felt after his death. "My parents had each other, but I was alone."

One student related the painting of Mary spanking the Christ child (Figure 71) to her own life's transition. Another couldn't say why it "impacted" on her so strongly. She thought it had to do with the strength of its line and color and the fact that "it turned something on its head." What was being suggested about the Christian icon, the Madonna, by garbing her in red, a color associated with anger and power, rather than in the more spiritual and traditional blue?

The largest percentage of the class chose photographs from *Gramp* (Figures 64–66, 96, 107, 114). The following reasons were given: the helplessness and dependency common both to infants and aged; reminiscences of grandparents' deaths; *memento mori* ("With babies we realize that we were once like they, with the elderly or chronically ill persons; the intimation of what's in store for oneself.") Another student commented on the final juxtaposition (Figures 114, 64): "It depicted the cycle of life so poignantly to me, showing how at birth and death we are all dependent on caregivers and the overwhelming power of love at both these junctures." Another student added, "The only certainty they have is death, as opposed to a baby's certainty (hopefully) of life." She found these images most memorable because they showed the importance of caring and helping one another over different thresholds—into and out of—life.

At the conclusion of the session, the group was asked whether anyone would have greater tolerance for the lingering death. Several said they might. One student wrote, "I voted for having a quick, sudden death, but now I'm starting to change my mind. I'm coming to see the importance of process, the time to share experiences."

RESPONSES OF MEDICAL STUDENTS, UNIVERSITY OF MASSACHUSETTS MEDICAL SCHOOL, WORCESTER, MA

Several weeks before entering medical school, members of the first-year class were sent a letter inviting them to devise and explain an image of any sort relating to their thoughts or feelings in anticipation of the experience of human dissection, which they would be performing for most of the year in their anatomy course. Twenty-nine images with descriptions were received, and several were worked into my introductory lecture, "Facing Dissection."

Examination of the responses reveals a curiosity about the source of the cadavers and their prior lives, apprehension and excitement about dissection, and concern about the students' own competence, callousness, and sensitivity.

Many of the images and accompanying explanations expressed appreciation to the body donors for "giving birth to our medical education" and "honoring us with the nakedness of their innerworkings." Others admitted to curiosity about, as well as respect for, the identity of the person who donated her or his body:

My God! She can't be any older than 30 . . . I'll bet she has children . . . Who's taking care of them now (Figure 135).

My drawing (not too artistic) is of a matronly woman whom I envision as having the type of personality necessary to have decided to donate her body to medical science (Figure 136). I just think about the anonymous (to me) person who was probably not quite so anonymous during his/her lifetime.

Figure 135.

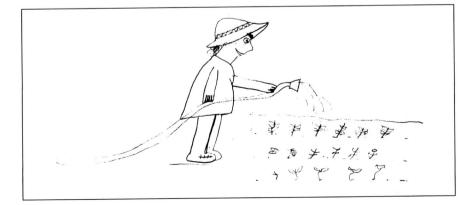

Figure 136.

A number of students depicted their own religious attitudes (Figures 137–139). The cross appears in two images, evidencing their particular faiths and concern for the whereabouts of the soul. They offered comments such as, "As a person who believes in an afterlife, I believe that many of the bodies we will be working on came from people who lived troubled lives. I believe that in death they will achieve the peace that they lacked in life."

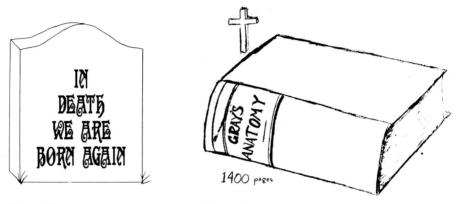

Figure 137.

Figure 138.

Figure 139.

Some reveal guilt. One student captioned a graphic of a skeletal figure holding his own outer skin (Figure 140): "It was not his own doing, it was mine," he wrote. Another admitted to suppressing a part of himself that would be horrified at what he is doing.

Still another apologized for not feeling guilty. His drawing (Figure 141) had two parts: an empty square labeled "image," underneath which a bearded man points accusingly, shedding a tear. A Catholic, this student supposes he should keep the lower image in his mind: "Does one really have the right to tamper with dead human beings?" The blank image signified the detachment he felt toward his prior experience dissecting animals. "The cadaver will be looked upon by me as an inanimate object rather than a once living, thinking, breathing human being. A callous attitude, for sure, but the truth."

Hoping I wouldn't find his relaxed attitude toward the notion of dissection too callous, one student apologized for not having composed an image. He did not view dissection of his own body for science or the betterment of another's life as being even remotely as distasteful as the conventional "modification" of his corpse by an undertaker, and he speculated that many anatomical gift donors might feel the same way. The thought of setting his first broken bone was more intimidating than cutting into his first cadaver.

It was not his own doing it was mine

Figure 140.

Figure 141.

Many exhibited what seemed like a "turning off" or "tuning out," by labeling anatomical parts or by drawing the body covered. As in the empty space image, the cadaver—itself a distancing word—is an object for instruction, a source of anatomical organs. One student explained that he did not view the cadaver as a formerly living being that once loved, cried, and laughed but rather as a composition of numerous components that worked together for the purpose of sustaining a human. Others drew the tools of their trade, acknowledging that even though the act of cutting may be seen as mutilation: "The scalpel cutting open a gash yields a marvelous sight into the unknown" (Figures 142–145).

Figure 142.

Figure 143.

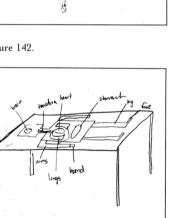

Figure 144.

Figure 145.

But the personhood of the cadaver constantly returned to focus. De-scribed as "the most uniquely human feature" and as "the identifying element conveying expression and emotion, the part of the body which is associated with a name, a personality, a self," the face is particularly evocative of dread, pity, and guilt. In two instances (Figures 146, 135) the face is presented literally covered. In Figure 147, it is the entire composi-tion. The artist wrote, "By no means can I conclude that without eyes and a smile (mouth) a human would cease to be human, but he/she would lose those features which to me indicate the source of life within."

One student saw personhood in the hand (Figure 148). Hoping not to become dehumanized in the process of medical education, he accompa-nied his image with a quotation from Ladd (*Ethical Issues Relating to Life and*

Death), which warns against the technocrat or biocrat physician seeing his patients only as "abstractions of etiology, diagnosis, and prognosis." Another admits awe at the entity of the organic structure: "This body represents an individual person (different from just a 'body') with character and spirit—none of which the most advanced psychiatrists or neurologists understand" (Figure 149).

Several students expressed anxiety about violating the body and particularly about their own competence (Figures 150, 151, 162, 163). One feared being observed in the act of mutilation: "Am I being watched by it as I cut, tear, and mutilate . . . ?" Still another was worried about being "an unskilled amateur anatomist." He drew an abstract representation of "the chaotic disconfiguration" created by the awkward probing of the naive first-year student, which "disturbs the linear representation of the human body as an organized, 'perfect' entity" (Figure 149).

Several students feared hurting the cadaver; others feared hurting themselves. A student commented, "I'm afraid that when I cut into the skin or an organ of a cadaver, that I'll feel the pain myself—which I hate! I can't imagine being able to do it!" (Figure 152). Self-probing about their own emotional reactions was also a common response "I will ask myself if I can do this so easily, are there other equally horrifying things I can do so easily?" one student queried. Even Figure 162, which speculates about death ("Death does come in many colors, but grey is so tragically common—a greyness which seeps under skin and into colorful eyes."), gives cause for questioning their role in connection to it. "Are we the defiant enemies of death or only the caretakers?" asked one respondent.

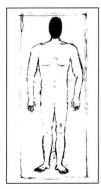

Figure 146.

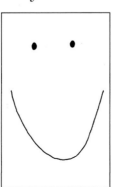

Figure 147.

Figure 148.

Figure 149.

Students recognized the importance of the desensitizing training of dissection as a way "to get the mind set to do what is necessary to save living patients in surgery or in emergency situations" (Figure 153, 154). Perhaps it is a wise tradition that the first patient with whom a medical student interacts is a dead one.

Seven students drew themselves in physical proximity to and discussed their interaction with the cadaver. Figure 155 was concerned with keeping the whole cadaver in view at all times: "To concentrate on a single feature would be to disrespect the whole human being to whom the body belonged." Acknowledging *intellectually* that the body is dead, this student could not entirely trust her emotional reaction. She wanted to be able to keep the whole cadaver in her sight for fear of not respecting its wholeness, and for fear it might move. Figure 156 depicts three medical students around the dissection table. The students and the cadaver all press their hands as if in prayer. The student wrote, "The students give thanks for the incredible experience which they are about to undertake. The cadaver asks

Figure 150.

only that his body be respected." Another image and commentary questioned (Figure 157) "What if that somewhere along the way, the body donor had some doubt or even at the last minute changed his mind. What does that make me?"

Several images, simultaneously address more symbolically many of these concerns: mutilation, self-consciousness,

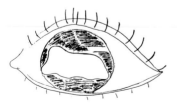

Figure 151.

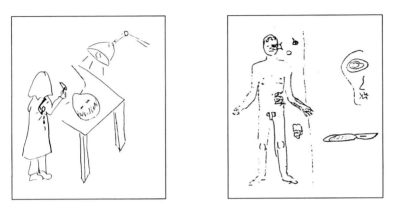

Figure 152.   Figure 153.

the whereabouts of the soul, the excitement in the knowledge to be gained. Two of the student artists wrote

> The body, ready for dissection, is a multi-layered, multi-colored box with its heart hidden deep inside. My hand, yellow with fear, lifted over the corpse, is ready to take hold of the knife, to cut through the body's layers in order to understand its structure. The spirit of the body has long ago flown free (Figure 158).

> . . . The blue edge around the whole form represents several things: death—cool, clean in the sense of a definite break—with the possibility of peace that comes from returning to the universe of undifferentiated energy. It also represents the sterile, cold, steely environment against which the dead body now rests. And finally, the cool detachment (at best) and self-protected denial (at worst) that I imagine all of us students will bring to the experience . . . . Through this blue boundary, we enter into the wonder and mysteries of the human body (Figure 159).

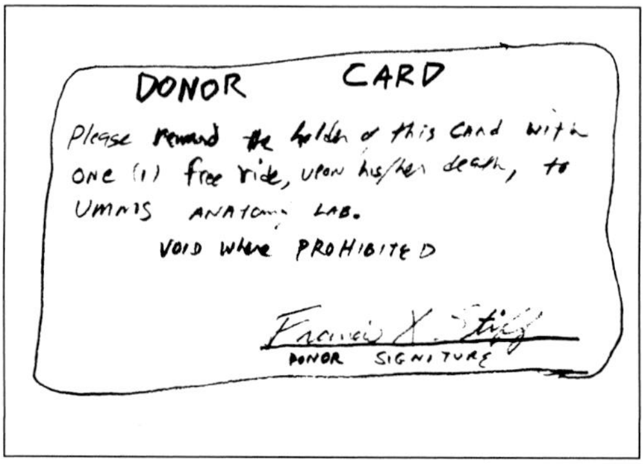

Figure 154.

Figure 155.

Figure 156.

Figure 157.

Figure 158.

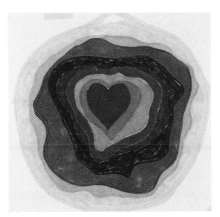

Figure 159.   Figure 160.

Figure 160, based roughly on the Chinese yin-yang symbol, represents the balance between antithetical elements of dissection. The artist wrote, "The upper right light symbol, a candle, suggests life-giving contrast to the pebbles of the lower left. The human body is incorporated into the center symbol to signify the focus of the conflict: the balance between opposites, beauty versus repulsion, loss of person vs. the dignity of donating one's body."

Some of the students' images are manifestly sensual, describing the sounds ("a place that was so quiet it was deafening") (Figure 161) and the odors ("one of my main concerns . . . was the smell of the formaldehyde we would encounter") (Figures 162, 151). "By exaggerating the nostrils, I emphasize the olfactory components of live bodies vs. cadavers. The intimate link between scent and memory gives us strong impressions of both live and dead scents" (Figure 160).

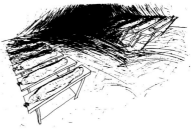

Figure 161.

One student mentioned a sense of isolation in being with the body "totally alone. Not frightened; just alone." One of the older students in the class admitted to feeling personally threatened and aware of her own mortality. She did not want a young corpse assigned to her because it would remind her that not just old people die. It would evoke the realization that she, herself, like the 30-year-old mother with children, could wind up on a lab table "leaving all her unfinished business behind." She identified the medical student in her drawing (Figure 135) as herself and admitted to having transferred her own fears and issues onto the cadaver.

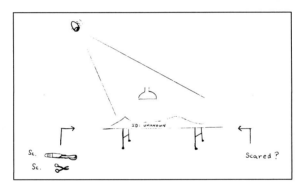

Figure 163.

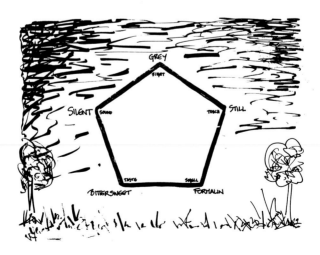

Figure 162.

The concerns expressed by most of the students were summarized fairly thoroughly by the verbal collage presented by one student (Figure 164).

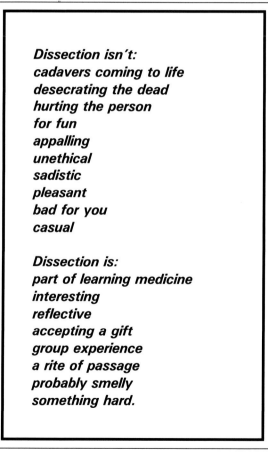

Figure 164.

• • •

The medical students' first lecture, "Facing Dissection," was a double-slide program that incorporated several of the students' own images created before the class, and introduced the history of dissection as portrayed through painting and literature, a description of the body donor program, and defenses and coping strategies. The lecture stressed the interdependence of art and science in medicine, citing instances of professional limitation resulting from suppressing emotions in training and clinical practice. The Death Attitude Questionnaire was distributed during that lecture.

Several weeks later the images in Chapter 2 were presented under the title "Facing Death: Caring and Coping." Intended to stimulate thought about death in contexts other than dissection, this lecture served as the stimulus for small group discussions facilitated by clinical and anatomy faculty. I met individually with faculty preceptors to suggest guidelines for responding to questions that might emerge during those discussions.

The medical students were asked to comment in writing on the image they found most memorable, either from the slides or packets of readings assigned in the module (see Appendix 2). Considering that the module primarily addresses the dissection experience, it was no surprise that the great majority chose images from the first presentation, "Facing Dissection." However, only reactions to images selected from those shown in the second lecture will be considered here. The Guidelines for Using the Arts (Chapter 4) offers a few examples of how student images were incorporated into the "Facing Dissection" presentation and how such images might be used in the future.

• • •

MOST MEMORABLE IMAGE

There was a large variation in responses from the 65 students who completed the most memorable image assignment. As in the other populations, the participants selected images from pop-culture, photographs, and the classical repertoire including those depicting the afterlife or portraying consoling or disturbing renditions of the dying experience.

One student was somewhat disturbed by the idealized scene in *The Death of Socrates* (Figure 5) because it did not harmonize with his personal experience. The student felt this image of Socrates failed to reflect the true consequences of death: "For Socrates," he wrote, "death is an intellectual exercise. His mourners are the ones who will bear the grief and pain of what will follow, namely the departure of life from the body of Socrates." Considering this image in the context of the dissection lab, where "the contrast between a living, thinking human being and a lifeless body is never more apparent," he concluded, "there seems nothing particularly noble in the death of a great philosopher when death means the loss of the mind and body which sustained his genius."

This student's small group had discussed whether death could ever be considered a dignified event. The student expressed appreciation for the clinical facilitator's sharing of his experience and point of view which concurred with his own. "Our physician seemed to think that in his specialty (pediatrics), it was difficult to accept the idea that death could ever be compatible with the concept of 'dignity.' We raised a number of questions which seemed to defy any quick solutions. The discussion was an excellent way to conclude the presentation. I welcomed the input of a physician who has to deal with the issues surrounding the death of a patient."

The theme of a dignified event, as opposed to a humiliating experience, was the reason another student chose the Cummings poem, "dying is fine/but death" (Figure 15). Contrasting the experience of the previously mentioned student with what he perceived as the medical school's view of dying (i.e., "a horrible process . . . to be prevented at any cost"), Cummings is viewed as presenting the dying process as "something good." The student found it hard to accept the processes of dying as "miraculous"—a term usually reserved for describing life. But he found Cummings's view on embracing dying as "lively," refreshing, contrary to how he usually feels about dying and how he had been taught to think about dying as a ". . . painful, sad, and humiliating termination." "Cummings," he wrote, "equates science with evil in describing death," and, adding that hospitals are places of science, the student found difficulty in reconciling science and emotion: "Just as Spock on *Star Trek* rejected emotion as debilitating to the scientific mind, so it seems with many true scientists—doctors being one kind of scientist. Spock was an efficient scientist, but who would want him as their family doctor?" The student's thoughtful commentary did not end here. Asked to note when in the dissection experience the "most memorable image" assignment was completed, the student reported that the poem held more significance when the anatomy course was nearly over. In Cummings's language, he puns:

I think that death in the lab has to be viewed "artificially" and "scientifically." Of course, there were times when it seemed appropriate to view the cadaver as a human being who had lived once and who could feel as we do now, and those were moments of sadness and awe. The uncovering of this person's face was one of those times. But our feelings about the cadaver couldn't help us learn anatomy, which in time will allow us perhaps to prevent many deaths. However, when it comes to the process of dying, I think it is important to use feeling as a way of letting patients know they are alive, since, as I think Cummings would agree, feeling really is living. It seems that in certain circumstances, medicine has not accepted dying, but has accepted death. I think, that as a medical student, this observation of death and dying by Cummings is somewhat startling, but so very vital to our understanding of ourselves.

Three students commented on images portraying immortality or afterlife. The slide of Buddha meditating peacefully (Figure 30) symbolized the cycle of life and rebirth to a Jewish student who believed death to be the transition period when one's soul does not inhabit a bodily form. For her, death is a time for reflecting on one's past Karma to determine what lessons are important to learn in the next life. Her belief in reincarnation thus made the dissection experience "an enjoyable one. While I respect the cadaver our group is working on, I believe that the body was simply a temporary vehicle by which a particular soul was expressing itself."

One student selected the Wyeth painting (Figure 39), commenting, "The pastel coloration and the fine lines of the artistry conveyed an impression of human form, in death, melding peacefully with the inanimate materials of nature." She chose this image as an ideal representation of death—"no struggles, a sense of naturalness and dignity, even perhaps a strange beauty, not of death itself but that of the 'big picture' that it is part of." She added, however, that thinking deeply about death was new to her and that she was emotionally uncomfortable with some of the images presented:

> Although I realize that coming to grips with death is a reality in becoming a physician, emoting in response to distressing images is a tough way to start the process. . . . Someday, perhaps sooner than I think, I will have had personal witness to

death to the extent that I rethink the ideal of the image in the painting. Whatever happens, I believe it may be helpful to keep that ideal there, and use the experiences I gain to bridge that ideal with reality. The real challenge, I think, will be making the connections in the middle, between the pain of the moment and the comfort of an image once held.

Also stimulated by the afterlife images, a third student described a new belief that the end of earthly existence is the beginning of a nonmortal, unearthly immortality. This thought could now help her to accept the notion of her death more easily. She expressed a strong belief in fate: "There are no accidents in life . . . everything happens for a reason"; yet she struggled with the idea:

> Philosophically, I can believe that there is a reason why an innocent mother and her two children were murdered in Townsend 2 weeks ago, but right now, that only makes it slightly easier to swallow—and I don't know if I could keep my faith at all if I were the husband who was the sole survivor of the family. I guess the bottom line for anyone is to have some concept of faith, to be able to cope with issues of death for which there is a reason, but one which we may not be able to recognize yet.

Images portraying isolation of the dying were most memorable to three students. Regarding Munch's *Death in the Sick Chamber* (Figure 92), one student referred more strongly to the lack of emotional communication in the painting than to the physical isolation. His commentary connected this image with the recent experience of his grandfather's death from cancer:

> Despite my frequent conversations and airplane visits to see him, I never talked to him specifically about his dying, even though this subject must have preoccupied him. I was surprised at my reluctance, given that death is not a frightening concept to me. Even when he would indirectly broach the subject of his death, I would consciously fail to recognize his cues. I was completely at ease when in physical proximity to my dying

grandfather, but I lacked the courage to be in emotional proximity. I wish that I had been less reluctant to really talk with
my grandfather. I will never have another opportunity.

The emotional distancing between the dying and the living was the
reason another student chose a scene from *The Shadow Box* (Figure 47).
She, too, considered the scenario in light of her own personal experience:

> . . . my mother's mother suffered from a series of cancers and
> heart problems over two to three years. She was psychologi-
> cally isolated with her pain and fears, not because of any lack
> of desire on her part or the parts of her husband and family to
> connect with one another and share her experience. Rather, it
> was an inability to transcend established patterns of communi-
> cation and behavior that kept the dying woman trapped in a
> separate existence. Even worse, as cancer encroached upon her
> brain, my grandmother underwent a marked personality
> change. A woman who had spent her life loving and caring for
> others became angry and abusive, at times pushing others
> away, her husband in particular . . . . While not as extreme, my
> grandfather's lingering death was also an isolating experience.
> A series of strokes and heart attacks that began as Grandma
> was dying claimed his life in the course of a year. He was
> depressed and lonely, even though in the midst of caring family.
> Perhaps a good candidate for psychological counseling, he
> never would have availed himself of it had the option even been
> offered.

She concluded with her belief that the deaths she experienced were "un-
fortunately typical; it is a rare event when death is realized as an opportunity for communication and growth."

A third student chose (Figure 50) to address this theme of isolation.
Initially amused by the humor in this get-well card, he realized the disturbing truth it expressed:

> If one visits a hospital or nursing home, one finds that a
> particular group of society, the elderly, are left unattended by

family and friends to suffer and eventually die. The elderly, which comprise a large percentage of the patient population, are often seen deposited at the doors of medical institutions and other health care facilities. Medical professionals are left to struggle to care for the elderly who are often tired, depressed, and impoverished. Because these lonely patients receive little emotional support, their illnesses linger on and their stay at the hospital lengthens. The elderly soon become a time, energy, and financial burden on medical personnel and facilities. It seems with the proper attention from family members, the patients would receive the motivation necessary to heal and recuperate.

A fourth student addressed the isolation theme in context of the photojournal, *Gramp* (Figures 64, 65, 114). Struck by the uncommon dedication the young man showed his grandfather during his time of dying, the student wrote:

> Cases of battered, abandoned, and forgotten old aged predominate our news as nursing home populations continue to rise . . . . The sick and dying in our society are the ones who need human contact the most. Not so much for the care they need from the health profession, but friendly contact with some love mixed in to keep them from feelings of loneliness, isolation and despair. As this young man so respectfully shows, the responsibility should be taken up by the family. It is a sign of failing family values in our culture when a majority of our elders are sent off to 'homes,' sometimes with few visits, to die in the midst of strangers.

Many other students chose images from *Gramp* because these photographs somehow echoed or contrasted with their own experiences with grandparents. One student felt guilty about how upsetting her grandfather's senility and death seemed to her at age 15. His deteriorating status frightened her so much that she rarely visited. "Seeing the slides reminded me of all that, and I had to leave the room at that point to keep from bursting into tears."

This same series of images stimulated quite an opposite recollection of a maternal grandmother in another student:

> She died over five years ago and yet certain memories of my time with her will remain with me forever. I remember the time when she held me, as a six year old, while we were in a ferry boat leaving China for Hong Kong. I remember going to the market with her, always expectant of a treat and never disappointed, be it a fresh ripe tomato, or some fresh sugar cane juice . . . She was the anchor, the center of our family. Her strength of character and authority enriched all those close to her, not only her immediate family, but neighbors from the same village where she came from, neighbors at the Hong Kong apartment building where she lived. Then the day came when she moved to Canada to be with my grandfather after years of separation. The immigration laws finally changed and made her dream come true.
>
> Then in the intervening years, we went our separate ways. In my own efforts to grow, I felt it necessary or needed to stretch in new directions; make new connections. I was always reassured at family gatherings that she was there, still, the magnet that held us together. It was indeed a shock when we heard that she had colon cancer. She fought to the end, as I knew she would, but to no avail. Near the end, she was defiant and yet vulnerable, and we, her children and grandchildren, only wished we had her strength and power, to care for and to comfort her in ways we learned from her. It is ironic that my sharpest memories are those of her in deep pain and anger, fighting the end of her tenure on earth. For her greatest gifts to me were those moments of sweet peace and comfort, when she taught me by example the many joys and possibilities in life.

Another student wrote of the image (Figure 64) of the young man cradling the grandfather in his arms. The image held particular meaning for the student during a subsequent visit with his parents:

> . . . I pictured myself as that young man holding my dying father. This visit forced me to come to terms with the fact that,

one day, I will have to face my parents' demise. And it was during that visit that I noticed, more than ever, their aged status. I can honestly say that following this presentation, I appreciate my parents' presence that much more.

The juxtaposition of grandfather holding grandson/grandson holding grandfather (Figures 114, 64) touched one student because of what he referred to as its "authenticity":

These [photographs] were not abstract thoughts or creative artwork attempting to capture a piece of reality, but reality itself, and as such unignorable. Our whole lives we are taught that death is 'bad,' that it should be pushed away, kept far away from (everyday) life, ignored and denied as much as possible. However, those photographs reminded me that death is natural and unavoidable in life. The photographs also exemplify the fears we hold about dying, of regressing, of being weak and helpless in the face of the inevitability of death . . . Above and beyond thoughts of death and dying, these images remind me of life, of the part of my life that is intrinsically real and important, and the part that is not. And sadly, it seems that it is the part that is not which takes up most of my time and energy.

Melville's image of unwashed tears blocking the healing stream (Figure 72) offered a timely balm for a student whose mother had died unexpectedly the third week of his first term in medical school:

I returned to medical school four days after my mother's funeral and was involved with an even greater work load and an even larger set of emotions than when I left.

For a short time, I was able to work at the same pace I had worked prior to my mother's death. However, about the time of the slide presentation I noticed I was very exhausted. When the slide flashed on the screen "Unwashed tears block the healing stream," it made me realize that I hadn't had any space since my mother's death to allow myself to grieve and experience the aftermath of emotions associated with her death. I wondered how I would continue to cope with the stress of medical school without really having any time to grieve . . . .

Anatomy was presenting the greatest difficulty for me academically and emotionally. To master the large amount of technical information required a consistent memory which was a problem for me. Performing the dissection continued to remind me at a subconscious level of the fact that I recently experienced a significant death in my life but had not spent enough time with my own feelings concerning that death. . . . It became very apparent to me in early November that I needed to unblock "the healing stream" by creating enough space for myself to grieve.

Slowly, I began to respond to the space and time. I began to grieve. I didn't articulate very many thoughts during this time, but I did sit still and think. Later I began to cry. I learned that the time I spent with my mother, who was comatose and on her death-bed, needed to be experienced in a reflective mood over time. I could not "explain away" or compartmentalize her death and put all my time into work . . . . My first real experience with death meant too much to me to ignore. Having allowed myself time to grieve, I began to realize in a way I had never before that

death is

the end of life.

By allowing himself space and time to grieve, the student concluded that he avoided

a very bad habit of ignoring major issues in my life: Grieving can be postponed but it can not be avoided. If postponed for too long a period of time, it can result in an emotional impairment and if a physician carries that impairment, it results in an impaired physician.

I am glad that I have been able to unblock and therefore partake of the healing stream.

Three students chose photographs of people living out their final days and hours on the palliative care service (Figures 110–113). One chose the cancer patient's wedding (Figures 110, 111): "The event portrayed a wonderful celebration of life and death. Marriage beautifully combines these two opposite events—'til death do us part.' " The student sensed great warmth and appreciation for the groom "willing to marry a dying woman—to comfort her 'in sickness and in health . . . as long as we both shall live.' . . . That man was going to support his wife through a horrendous ordeal, comfort her physically and emotionally and at the same time feel the pain himself, probably without receiving comfort and compassion in return."

The student did not relate this experience in any way to her cadaver or dissection, but she did acknowledge having gained an "object lesson," an insight into this groom's action and the practice of medicine:

> We will become involved with dying patients, belligerent patients, and emotionally crippled patients, and yet we will have to go on practicing. The patient in Room 10 may have just lost her child in labor, and we will have to grieve with her, and then shortly thereafter celebrate the joy of the mother in Room 12 who has just given birth to a healthy son.

Two students responded to the photograph of four generations at the deathbed (Figures 112, 113). One mentioned that the photograph underscored the notion that "dying time is truly living time":

> Although I found this illustration very striking, the theme arising from this picture which impressed me most was that of 'living until you die.' The patient is obviously very sick; he appears very thin and frail. Indeed, we were told that the patient died several hours after this photograph was taken. Yet, despite his proximity to death, he is still very much alive. The joy he is experiencing in seeing this baby is evident on his face, and he is even able to physically reach out to the child. It is also apparent that this man's loved ones are still treating him as if he is very much alive. The fact that they have brought this baby in to see the patient shows that they have not withdrawn

from him but instead are still sharing their lives with him. To me this scene is a wonderful depiction of the concept that we are either alive or dead, not living or dying.

The other student chose the same photographs because it evoked a personal experience:

> Death is not an unfamiliar face to me. My father died when I was twenty (eleven years ago). I find that I am still grieving—but at unexpected times and in unexpected ways. Many of the images I've seen have made an unforgettable impression. During the second slide presentation, I wanted to flee the room because my throat already had such a large unswallowable lump in it, and I didn't want to face such difficult stuff. I found that I couldn't prevent the tears from leaking out. When I saw the image of the dying man with members of the family and close friends gathered around to make their peace and say goodbye, I thought, what a wonderful but hard way to say that final goodbye. Oh, how I wish that we could have been there like that for my father. He died alone. The guilt that remains will probably never completely fade although I do feel that my father understands that he is/was very loved.

Still another student, recalling the poem written by a young girl on the occasion of her grandfather's death (Figure 52), wrote:

> I was 18 when my grandfather (my mother's father) died. He died 3 or 4 days post-op of complications from an operation, so the family had not endured any long suffering yet was somewhat alerted to the fact that he might not recover. He is the first close relative of mine who has passed away. . . . At the funeral, the priest gave a long eulogy, and people began to pay their respects to the deceased. My grandmother took me to see my grandfather's body. She looked cheery and bright as she always does and she said to me, 'See Grampy, doesn't he look beautiful.' He was all made up and wearing his "best suit" and she was right—he looked better than he had in years. Somehow, though, that seemed an inappropriate statement to me. I

justify it by knowing that my grandmother is deeply religious and God's taking my grandfather was to her merely His way. She, in essence, was not sad but happy for my grandfather . . . . I remember my mother crying intermittently from the time my grandfather died to the burial, and all the while telling my brother and me that it was the best thing that could have happened; that he would suffer and struggle no more. This to me seemed an appropriate cross of emotion and scientific reason. Mom was sorry or sad to lose her beloved father, but she knew medically his options and problems with continuing to live.

As for me, I play the role of the child in the quote. I do not remember crying or even feeling like crying was necessary. In a sense the funeral was a family reunion and I remember thinking it odd that relatives who hadn't seen one another in a long time sat around the room conversing as if nothing was wrong or was in the least bit different.

I guess it was a mix of feelings I had that day. I understood medically that what had happened was "good," yet I felt the loss as my mother did. In fact I remember trying to put myself in her shoes, as if it were my dad that had died—boy, did that bring tears to my eyes.

One student's most memorable image derived not from the presentation but rather from her small group discussion afterward. She felt some individuals in her group were upset by the presentation, and expressed this as anger or frustration with the format of the presentation and the small group discussion. Her description is touching:

Two of the members of the group began discussing recent losses they had suffered and not yet grieved because of the demands of school. One woman began to cry and was quite embarrassed by it. Her father had died just before school started. Another woman left the room because she started to cry. The most interesting moment from my perspective was when another woman went over to comfort the student who had lost her father. She is normally a very unemotional person; she presents herself as irritated with the world, and although she was clearly angered by the fact that emotions she preferred to ignore were aroused, she was sympathetic to another person who was hurting. I think that the reason this has stuck with me all this time is that it demonstrated both how different people react to their own emotions and to the emotion of others with shame, anger, frustration, sympathy and compassion at the same time. I tend to be very open and accepting of unpleasant emotions in myself and others so it was a different perspective that was shown to me.

● ● ●

The intent of this module was to give medical students a place to address their concerns in a relaxed, nonjudgmental atmosphere. With their peers, anatomy instructors and clinicians, they talked about anxieties, inhibitions, and vulnerabilities. Their responses to the slide presentation indicated compassion, thoughtfulness, and, in some cases, enabled them to bring personal grief to the surface.

In addition to curiosity and the excitement of investigating the blueprint provided by the cadaver, human dissection raises unsettling concerns—in particular, performing acts that one would regard inconceivable under *any* circumstances. Obviously, physicians cannot be so traumatized by emotional feelings that they are unable to intervene surgically—even to amputate—or provide other therapy in the name of restoring health. However awkwardly it is labeled, "detached concern," "mature concern," or "appropriate emotional armor" is a critical skill to be mastered by the medical student. Nevertheless facing and expressing the aversions, fears, and fantasies associated with human dissection and death—acknowledging that personal reactions are neither trivial nor to be suppressed, denied, or ignored—helps prepare the student not only for academic work in the anatomy laboratory but also for the emotional work that patient care or the "laying on of hands" requires.

RESPONSES OF GRADUATE NURSES, UNIVERSITY OF MASSACHUSETTS SCHOOL OF NURSING, BOSTON, MA

The population was comprised of 10 experienced nurses and nursing supervisors drawn from geriatric facilities in Massachusetts, all students in a graduate program at the School of Nursing, University of Massachusetts-Harbor Campus, Boston. Ages ranged from 21 to 58 years. A week before the 3-hour seminar, members were asked to create an image related to their attitude toward or concerns about death. Six of the ten members of the class completed the assignment. The Death Attitude Questionnaire was administered the day the program was presented. Discussion preceded and followed the double-slide presentation of images. During the break, participants were asked to complete the "most memorable image" form.

One participant created a collage; the others used either pen or pencil. Themes included concrete interpretations of fear, afterlife, sleep, and sadness as well as abstract representations of life and unity.

The director of a geriatric nursing facility identified death as the major source of anxiety in her work. She believed that if her patients and staff can learn to see death as a natural event and discuss it, they can begin to appreciate the present. Her image (Figure 165) simply presented the life-death cycle as a continuum: a circle composed of arc-shaped arrows indicating different developmental stages with death as the ending. Underneath, joined hands captioned "touching during dying" added a human component to the abstract form.

Figure 165.

A second image (Figure 166) also depicted death and life in an abstract form and as inextricably connected. The spokes seem to represent the ever-changing, ever-evolving manifestations of death. According to the artist, the blank, unlabeled spoke could accommodate a future thought or dimension since, during life, the vision remains incomplete. Like the arrows of the geriatrician, the divisions between the spokes were not intended to be viewed as distinct, separate entities. The artist suggests that

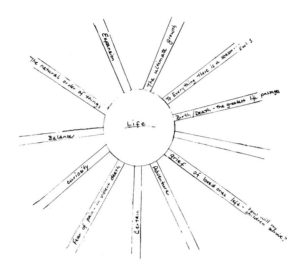

Figure 166.

they should be seen as flowing into each other. "Facing death is many thoughts at once—all part of a whole which is greater than and unexplainable by the sum of its parts." The nurse added that with the exception of intense colors for fear and grief, she would have colored this picture "mostly soft, peaceful colors . . . the ultimate growth and expansion would be bright (yellow probably)."

An Asian nurse also arranged representational images in a circular form (Figure 167). She composed a collage of scenes from family life—a life cycle of sorts: children playing in their rooms, a man in bed, a woman in bed, a phrase "peaceful and calm." According to her religious beliefs, every person goes into the world with a special mission which begins at birth. Birth, growing old, death, and separation from loved ones are all fulfillment of one's "desires or mission of whole" from beginning to end. In the Eastern philosophy, death is the symbol for transition, rebirth or reincarnation into one's next mission in the world. She concluded that when she must face death, she will feel calm and peaceful because she will

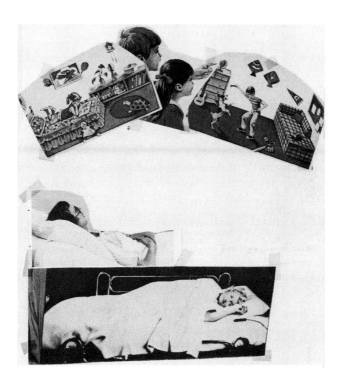

Figure 167.

have finished her one assigned mission and will be looking forward to the next.

Contrasting sharply with the tranquility of the previous three images, one group member sketched an interpretation of Edvard Munch's *The Shriek*, an isolated form crying out in anguish and loneliness (Figure 168).

Two nurses drew representations of their own deaths. In Figure 169, the nurse pictured herself as a young woman at the edge of a precipice, poised to step off into a chasm of wavy lines. Provocative elements include the moon surrounded by four stars and the pathway, behind her, which lead the viewers eyes upward. Her commentary discussed the two paths and why she chose to follow the one symbolizing death. She envisioned herself dying suddenly "alone . . . dark . . . unexpected." She predicted this sort of death for herself because her father died suddenly at

Figure 168.   Figure 169.

age 49 followed by similar deaths of several of his brothers and sisters: "It probably is a better death than a chronic illness," she explains, "but it does create a traumatic impact on those left behind. My father has been dead now for twenty years, but I still remember his death very clearly—like it was yesterday."

In Figure 170 another nurse expressed concern with the traumatic effect her death would have on those left behind. She drew her husband and two young children at her gravesite in front of their home. Shielded from view by the clouds, she watches them from above. Literally portraying her helplessness, this scene represents her greatest fear—that her young children will be left without a mother: "It saddens me to think they would not have my physical presence. I do believe that even dead, I would be able to see them, but it would be awful not to be able to comfort my husband and children in so much pain."

• • •

Figure 170.

The Death Attitude Questionnaire was completed by all of the 10 nurses in attendance on the day of the class. They were then asked to choose between sudden death or a lingering terminal illness. The group response was relatively equally divided. Those who chose sudden death expressed a desire to be spared pain and financial burden. Some had seen "good" sudden deaths in home and hospital settings. An example was provided by a supervisor of a Lifeline Program. (Lifeline is an electronic device that provides 24-hour response from the telephone of a person who lives alone to a responder usually linked to a hospital or other healthcare facility.) She had become close to an elderly female "patient" over a period of 18 months, and discovered her client dead on a home visit. The woman was dressed, sitting in a chair, legs crossed, apparently enjoying a pear. The woman had been able to continue to live independently because she had enjoyed the security of the lifeline.

Another nurse described the doom phenomenon—"the forewarning of death.'" An aged woman, recuperating in a hospital setting from minor surgery, reported she just felt strange. Recognizing the phenomenon, the nurse in charge was able to assign someone to the patient immediately. Shortly thereafter the patient suffered a massive embolism. The nurse reported with pride that the woman's last memory was not falling unconscious to the floor but having her hand held.

The lingering death was selected by other participants to give time for farewells, especially to family members. One class member reported she was keeping a diary of thoughts and feelings for her daughters should sudden death occur or serious illness result in a coma. Another described a role model in the Orient, who celebrated her 80th birthday and every birthday thereafter by repainting her coffin which she had purchased years earlier. When the elderly woman lost her teeth, she placed them in the coffin, a practice not unlike the Orthodox Jewish custom of burying an amputated limb to be joined by the remainder of the body at the time of death.

MOST MEMORABLE IMAGE

Two members of the group identified *The Death of Socrates* (Figure 5) as their most memorable image—one because it allowed time for goodbyes; the other, the youngest member of the group, thought it expressed "elan." Though suicide is contrary to her ethos, she writes, she chose this image because in essence it is the way she would prefer to die.

The Robinson photograph, *Fading Away* (Figure 8), was chosen as most memorable by a nursing supervisor because it related both to her professional and personal life. She finds her work—helping older people come to terms with death and dying—fulfilling, but finds it painful to think of young people dying. Between the grief work she has done with patients and bereaved parents and her own feelings as a mother of four growing children, she admits, "This is the most difficult."

One nurse selected the passage about the intern forcing the husband out of the hospital room at the moment of death (Figure 93) as her greatest fear. She herself had been able to defy the hospital authorities to arrange for her parents' needs during the last 10 days of her father's life. Despite the success of her efforts, which she equated with those described in *Last Letter to the Pebble People* (Figure 101), she felt that a part of her died last year with her father's death from lung cancer. She mentioned the close-up photograph from the Palliative Care Unit of the dying great-grandfather (Figure 113) and the grandson/Gramp scenes (Figures 114, 64). She recalled with pride how she was able to honor her father's last request to stand up a few hours before he died. She saw the same joy and light in his eyes that she sees in the eyes of the old man with the baby. She wrote, "And as I cared for his frail body, I understood the image of the grandson carrying Gramp."

Apologizing for not being able to limit herself to one most memorable image, she added the couplet "loving not enough/loving too much," from Spender's poem (Figure 76), a powerful, haunting feeling with which she continues to live. It seemed appropriate that her personal image (Figure 166) was the many-spoked sunburst, which epitomized her kaleidoscopic feelings surrounding the experience of death.

One image of afterlife (Figure 30) was chosen by the Asian nurse because it matched her theory of reincarnation. She also mentioned other images: *The Death of Socrates* (Figure 5) and the photograph of the young granddaughter at the bedside of *Gramp* (Figure 107) because they avoided neither death nor the saying of goodbyes. She saw and appreciated for the first time how a child can be given a chance to learn that dying and death are part of life's process.

Several other members of the class cited images from *Gramp* (Figures 64-66, 96, 99, 107, 114) because of their personal perspectives and the images' authenticity and poignancy. Some of the comments included the following: "the everyday stark contrasts of birth and death, young and old age, good health, sickness; and it goes on"; "The sense of despair, pain and resignation in Gramp's face ... It really captured the essence of several issues. I can't quite get it down on paper but the grandfather's face is so *full* of emotion. It's such a study. I'd like more time to just look at that face." "The [recent] birth of my daughter is perhaps what made this especially timely. I hold her now; will she hold me later? She is totally unbelievable to me. I may be [the same] to her at some point."

The quotation from *A Death of One's Own* (Figure 115)—the reciprocal nature of being someone's "blessing"—evoked interesting personal recollections for two nurses. Wrote one, "[It] recalls the most recent and most important loss—the death of my father and my closeness and help to him (and his to me)." The other commented, "I had the chance with many patients but most importantly with my stepfather. I knew he felt safer when I was there. It also made me smile—his last words were "oh shit." I would not have missed being there." She added, "It was the most important thing I have ever done. Now it's sad but so very consoling."

The nurse whose own drawing was an intentional copy of Munch's graphic, "The Shriek," referred to sharing her father's death and, at the same time, to the image from *Cancer Ward* of the father feeling walled off from his family (Figure 43). To her, the closeup of the open mouth of the dead man in the *Gramp/Gericaux* juxtaposition also suggested her father's isolation. Is it the open mouth, the projected content, or the resemblance to the silent scream in these images that cries out against the solitariness, the profound aloneness of dying?

The responses from this group demonstrate clearly that experience adds yet another dimension to the contemplation of death. These nurses had already had confrontations with death in their professional practice, and being older than the medical, college, and junior and senior high school students, many had already confronted death in their personal lives. Yet because of the environments in which they work, they felt they had not been able to "process" their experiences. For them, the slide presentation offered a way to release emotions that had been blocked and to work toward healing some of the pain they had suppressed. Clearly such a "catharsis" argues for the benefit of periodic inservice workshops that encourage even the most experienced professionals to be attentive to their own emotional barometers.

RESPONSES OF HOSPICE VOLUNTEERS, STATE-WIDE CONFERENCE, MASSACHUSETTS

The double-slide presentation was presented at an annual 1-day conference for volunteers, sponsored by the Hospice Federation of Massachusetts. After completing the Death Attitude Questionnaire, group members were invited to consider the death they would choose for themselves, a sudden death or a lingering illness. The majority chose sudden death, expressing a desire to spare themselves pain (primarily physical), and their families the emotional and financial burdens of providing care over a long period of time. No participant chose to die in a hospital, and no one preferred to be alone. Those who chose the lingering death did so to be able to prepare themselves and to be able to say goodbye to family members. After the formal presentation of images, members of the group completed the most memorable image handout.

Three volunteers chose images that demonstrated the isolation of the dying—the quotation from *Cancer Ward* (Figure 43), Munch's *Chamber of Death* (Figure 92), or Klimpt's *Spectre of Death* (Figure 42). One volunteer, a medical technician, expressed concern about walls between the dying and living, particularly in light of the AIDS crisis: "We tend sometimes to get so involved with disease that we forget the person." Another chose the image of isolation because, as a bereavement coordinator, she "continually works with the needs of hospice patients and families to communicate, so they can deal with their feelings and understand what is happening to them during the grief process."

Discussion centered on the problem of theory versus emotions: it is one thing to know intellectually that anger and sadness must be reckoned with; it is quite another matter to accomplish this grief work—that is, the acknowledgement and expression of one's deepest feelings. Accordingly, one volunteer chose the cartoon graphic "I Hate You" (Figure 70) because of its humor and honesty. She addressed the difficulty of translating theory and concepts into practice: "I am working with a great family . . . but I am unable (and so are other volunteers) to facilitate expression of feelings of anger which must be there." Another chose Melville's image of "tears unwashed" (Figure 72) as prototypic of unresolved grief. Unexpressed grief, she revealed, is part of her own "journey." Following a personal loss, she did not grieve well and had to consult a therapist. In her professional capacity as a volunteer and bereavement counselor in an elementary school, she also addressed the subject of facilitating grief work: "So many of my patients and their families have many stones upon their hearts. When we are able to reach them and enable them to remove the 'death wait (dead weight)' from their hearts, it is beautiful to observe the process of grief as it can rightfully resolve."

Several others chose as most memorable the cartoons, get-well cards, humorous epitaphs, and poems from popular culture (Figures 16, 22, 50, 51, 53). Two volunteers came to a new realization of the possibilities of these resources. The truth of the messages from such unlikely sources seemed to surface with freshness for two others because, behind the humor, they perceived serious thought, truth, ultimate meaning. In the card "We all hate to see you sick . . . So none of us are coming . . ." (Figure 50) this truth is borne out professionally "in patients AND families and validated, as well, in personal experience." In one situation in a volunteer's own family "two brothers were unable to accept—deal with, be with—the dying one."

One volunteer was amused by the card "Too bad you're sick but you have the will to carry on . . ." (Figure 53) because she knew people to whom this sentiment applied. In her commentary, she considered the serious implications of this concept in terms of cancer and reviewed the image in the context of her own family:

> Curiously enough, my husband often asks about a new patient assignment: 'Did they smoke,' etc. Even though we can't blame another for contracting an illness such as cancer, there are those people who do feel that way. My husband, by the way, is a runner and fairly health conscious. I can't imagine his reaction if he develops such an illness.

One volunteer chose the Price cartoon (Figure 88), seeing in it the idea of wanting to die together and finding the thought congruent with her personal belief: ". . . [A] married couple who lived together most or three-fourths of their lives, who had always done *everything* together, would want to die together . . . togetherness even in death, which is where my husband and I are at and have been all our lives."

Another group member said the cartoons eased the sorrow he experiences with patients at their deaths. We discussed the therapeutic value of laughter. Another volunteer commented on the greeting cards and their appropriateness for terminally ill persons. She mentioned the "grieving cards—both humorous and otherwise." We discussed the solace of such texts as "Your body may be failing you . . . but your spirit will go on forever," and the straightforward power of the plain, old-fashioned, hand-written words "My thoughts [prayers, love, etc.] are with you."

Photographs and paintings that exposed the graphic realities of death and dying were selected as most memorable to several group members. One volunteer was touched by Figure 78 because it reminded her of her own experience with her mother and "how caring for her personal needs was the most difficult for her." Another cited the Munch drawings (Figures 90, 92, 95) because of the realities they presented—"the loneliness, fear and unpleasant side of dying—something we all must understand and deal with underneath all the love and caring we bring to each patient and family we work with." She had particular difficulty coping with the dying person's odors, which persisted in her memory even after death had occurred. One volunteer expressed displeasure with the image of the Madonna spanking the Christ Child (Figure 71). She writes, "Somehow the idea of the Madonna out of control or angry at a helpless one is too distressing."

The moment of death section of the presentation was mentioned by several volunteers and chosen as most memorable by 6 participants. The close-up of Gramp juxtaposed against the Gericault painting (Figures 99, 100) triggered bittersweet memories. One volunteer was immediately reminded of a recent hospice situation that had a positive outcome: "It brought tears to my eyes . . . The man I helped had many unresolved family issues, and I was able to help him in several instances with his former wife. I urged her to see him and his eldest son. I sent word to the son to please visit and talk with his father soon. (He did.)" Another volunteer connected the photographs with the Lerner quotation (Figure 115). She saw in the faces of the dying men "the same look I had seen while being with a close friend (surrogate parent) at the moment of death. Being with the person, watching her die for seven hours was the hardest thing I have ever done, yet thinking of it as a blessing makes it easier." A third participant singled out the moment of death suggested by the Munch graphic juxtaposed against the quotation from *Last Letter to the Pebble People* (Figures 95, 77), commenting on how "physically and emotionally exhausting" tending to the dying is. Death in this instance would be relief: "When death comes at last—there is such a relief. The loved one is free."

Two volunteers chose Alice Walker's poem, "Medicine" (Figure 91). One wrote, "It brought home the importance of 'togetherness' to the end at the end." She advocated installing double beds in hospice wings to foster privacy and facilitate closeness. The other volunteer was touched by how the intimacy of death and the solace that a loved one can provide is expressed so eloquently by the Walker poem: "It's especially meaningful because I just got married and hope that I can be as much comfort to my husband as the woman in the poem was to hers. P.S. I have long braided hair, too!"

The intense closeness that is possible at the moment of death was the reason another volunteer chose Picasso's *The Kiss* (Figure 104):

> The union of the two sets of lips left me with a good sense of loving and sharing. The drawing showed much intimacy, even though only two heads and faces were shown. The faces remained attached at the lips even though the side of the female face could be seen. . . . Personally I couldn't help but think of my love for my husband. The lines on the faces made the two blend beautifully. As a volunteer, I can relate this Picasso work

of art to loving couples who are dealing with death and dying. There is much love.

Another volunteer saw a similar intimacy in the photograph of two children with cancer (Figure 86) and named it as most memorable:

> [It] just stayed with me. These two children seemed so happy to have found each other. I could instantly imagine them sharing their experiences with a rapport that neither could find in anyone else. I guess this image reaffirms my deep belief in our need for each other as human beings, and the importance of seeking those we can truly open our souls to. As a volunteer and just as one human being to another, I guess I'd like to open myself more and more to the limitless possibilities of sharing life's experiences.

Fifteen volunteers mentioned photographs from *Gramp* (Figures 64–67, 78, 96, 99, 107) and 10 chose these images as most memorable. The images of the grandson carrying the grandfather (Figure 64) were chosen by one volunteer because "the involvement during illness helps you communicate your love and caring." She wrote of the importance of helping a loved one die with dignity in a familiar setting with a caring family "not among strangers." She also expressed concern with facilitating the expression of anger and sadness. "We need to be guided in how to encourage families to care for their loved ones at home if the patient wishes to remain at home. All generations of the family should be encouraged to visit, care for, and speak of their life together and their love and caring before death."

For one volunteer, however, the image of the grandson carrying his grandfather in his arms confirmed her wish to die suddenly: "All the love and compassion that was evident in that image did not outweigh the lack of dignity for that old gentleman." Not unlike her colleague, who chose the photograph of him toileting tended to by a young family member (Figure 78), she would not like to see herself in this scenario, since her memory of caring for her own dying mother felt like a compromise in self-esteem.

Of the juxtaposition of images from *Gramp* (Figures 114, 64), several other volunteers made the following comments:

> Makes me think of 'what goes around, comes around'— that we need our family. The incredible irony of the two photos as feeling the irony of our lives, that we must lean on others and be ready to be leaned on, that we must give.

> The powerful visual effect; two pictures that say so much ... The importance of families to openly show their mutual love.

> [They] show how life in a family goes on. That the role of loving caretaker was reflected in each of the generations.

> ... comforting to me that the loving and caring survived the years; this does not always happen.

> The reminder of the reciprocity of care between the generations—even if it is the "stronger" holding your frail grandmother/grandfather.

Other most memorable images evoked for two volunteers a positive attitude toward death. One cited Anne Sexton's poem, "Courage" (Figure 4); David's *The Death of Socrates* (Figure 5) wrote the other, "would be great for patients to focus on during fearful times." Two volunteers chose Figure 41, which suggests transforming the deathbed into the bed of life by virtue of organ or tissue donation. Both identified personally with the tone of this piece as well as its content. Wrote one volunteer, "attributing value to life, but most importantly the burying of faults, prejudices, etc. Hopefully they may be gone by then, if I start now." Wrote the other, "It says precisely what I want to say upon dying."

The hospice group expressed surprise at the power and relevance of the literary and visual arts and appreciation for exposure to a previously unexplored territory. The participants resonated with and derived great insight and affirmation from the blend of serious and comic. Their parting comments summarized their freedom (new-found for some) to confront both positive and negative emotions in their volunteer work.

I have never seen, heard, or even considered the arts with respect to death and dying. Powerful presentation . . . wonderful, varied collection. Will now be more aware.

What a range of emotions . . . a marvelous way to allow each individual to experience each image personally, whatever way is relevant to them.

I appreciated the intermingling of laughter and tears. It's the way I experience life.

Very moving. Especially good mixture of humor and pain, sadness and joy. Thank You!

It was delightful and also very helpful in bringing many fragmented thoughts and images together. Personally, I find the release of many feelings through literature.

One member of our group expressed it very well by saying the presentation brought her back to her roots and why we became volunteers working with the terminally ill. It reinforced my joy.

DISCUSSION

The images presented to the five populations targeted many issues commonly identified in the clinical literature: communication difficulties between patients, staff, and family members; concern about the physical and emotional suffering; maintaining a sense of control; and the desire for both a dignified death and aftermath—a literal, social, spiritual, or theologic immortality.

The visuals were geared toward evoking emotional responses rather than intellectual, clinical, or rational reactions. The facilitator must be prepared for a full range of emotional reactions—from nervous laughter to tears, and should alert the group ahead of time to the potentially strong nature of the material. He or she needs to be available after the session to insure against members having nowhere to go with exposed wounds. In

each group the majority of participants discussed the images in relationship to deeply personal, poignant experiences with death. Even in the medical student population, where psychological resistance (objective conditioning) was strongest, participants often returned to subjective experience when asked to select a most memorable image.

Selected for their implicit humanistic bias, the images were intended to help participants identify their own concerns and beliefs, develop understanding, tolerance, compassion, and especially adaptive skills.

The goal in all presentations was to enable participants to relate to the images in personal terms. This method serves two purposes: it is both therapeutic in the way it allows previously unacknowledged grief to be vented, or known griefs to be re-viewed. As with support groups, using the arts in these ways allows participants to reflect on their own coping capacities and to note how far they have come in traversing both the rapids and the calm waters of grief. It also reminds us of the universality of the death experience and provides new resources to enhance understandings, skills, and comfort helpful for dealing with future instances of dying and death in both personal and professional spheres.

In examining the responses obtained from the five audiences who completed the Death Attitude Questionnaire and viewed the double-slide presentation, six areas of commonality and six areas of differences emerged:

Similarities

Most Distasteful Aspects of Dying

All respondents indicated that the most distasteful aspect of their own death was the grief it would cause to relatives and friends.

Concepts of Afterlife

No participant from any group expressed fear of a judgment in an afterlife. Interestingly, images of the afterlife were identified by many as most memorable, although several of these images were abstract or symbolic. This is probably peculiar to contemporary Western culture. As is commonly known, other cultures and other historical times have different perspectives on death.

Though they did not seem to fear a heavenly reckoning, most participants view death as being followed by a survival of the spirit. Only the medical students significantly viewed death as the end of existence. Such a finding may reflect a semantic difference among medical students with respect to the term "death" (i.e., a discrepancy between various literal, clinical definitions of death as opposed to spiritual or emotional definitions). However, the medical students' drawings in anticipation of dissection often portray a sense of being watched or of being judged, which could be interpreted as reflecting some type of belief in survival of the spirit.

Two of the junior and senior high school students were consoled by a vision of the heavens peopled with welcoming, recognizable Christian figures. Among the Lesley College students, two images of heaven from the presentation El Greco's *Burial of Count Orgaz* (Figure 25) and Picasso's *Evocation, The Burial of Casagemas* (Figure 31) were likened to their own; and 8 or more of the 19 images drawn before the double-slide presentation, where the mandate was to draw an image relating to their concerns about death—real or imagined, depicted the afterlife in some specific format.

Though skewed to view death in the context of their forthcoming dissection experience, 29 medical students incorporated images of afterlife in their drawings, either by indicating that the soul of the cadaver was living on, or depicting him or herself being watched by the deceased. Further, four medical students chose images relating to the afterlife as most memorable.

In the nurse population, three of the six drawings addressed the continuum and connectedness of death and life. One respondent envisioned herself after death watching her family grieve much like the medical students felt watched by their cadavers' spirits.

Not all of the images of the afterlife were as concrete. Some chose the more symbolic life-after-death images as evidenced by the Wyeth/Burroughs, anatomical gift, or cadaver donations (Figures 39–41). Selections of these images as most memorable reflect a view of afterlife more metaphoric, like Lifton's modes of symbolic or Morganthal's social immortality, where death is transcended not by one's body or spirit living on in another world but by the immortality of the world one left behind.

Attitudes Toward Autopsy

Very few participants strongly disapproved. Most people in every population either approve of the procedure or don't care. Four of the populations had little or no experience with autopsy. It is not their view of death and hence they do not find it necessary to take a strong stance.

Unique among these groups, the medical students, perhaps, cannot afford to disapprove of autopsy. The procedure is necessary not only for medical training but also for future medical research. They have committed themselves to a career that derives much of its knowledge base for diagnosis, treatment, and research from autopsies.

Organ Donation

The overwhelming majority of every population was not only willing to donate their hearts for transplantation after they died, but they would also donate them to any stranger who needed them. In the high school student group, 100% of the respondents were willing to do so. It is possible that such a donation and its implications are unknown to them or perhaps people answer such questions differently in the abstract. This assumption could be cross-checked by correlating the responses to two additional questions: (1) Do you have a donor card?; and (2) If your family were asked about an autopsy, would they allow it?

Most Memorable Image

The image most consistently selected as most memorable by all five populations was the concluding juxtaposition of the two photographs (Figures 114, 64). Perhaps this is because they are among the final images of the presentation and the finale plays a part in evoking such a response. But images from the *Gramp* series were most frequently cited in discussions by all populations. Thus, more significantly, these photos seem to reflect a universal hope for such compassion in their own future experience with dying among the five populations—in the real or ideal.

Differences

Concern with the Subject of Death

Although all populations report thinking about death occasionally, a larger percentage of the hospice workers and nurses reported that they think of death frequently. This difference reflects the nurses' roles as geriatric supervisors, and their work with the elderly in lifeline programs, nursing homes, or hospital settings. Hospice volunteers also work exclusively with dying persons and their families, so both of these groups are constantly confronting the imminence and reality of death. Junior and senior high school students probably think about death less because they are highly motivated by their past successes and future prospects.

Death Wishes

Although most participants reported that there was a time in their lives when they wanted to die, their reasons differed. Medical students cited periods of emotional turmoil or intolerable situations. Junior high school and senior high school students cited embarrassment as the precipitating factor. Curiously, among the Lesley College and medical student populations, no one cited physical pain as reason for wanting to die, yet this was a precipitating factor in the other three populations.

Body Disposition

On the question of the disposition of their own bodies, four populations were evenly split between the choice of cremation or burial. Among the junior and senior high school student group, the majority chose burial over other alternatives. This may reflect a lack of familiarity with other forms of disposition.

Types of Funerals

There was a great deal of variation in choice of funeral practices. Many hospice volunteers preferred not to have a funeral. I am surprised by this finding since the presentation and subsequent discussion so highly endorsed rituals of saying goodbye when death was imminent. The other four populations acknowledged the desire for a funeral but stipulated provisos. The junior-senior high school students voiced preferences for small funerals, attended by friends and relatives. Generally, nurses wanted a funeral but did not make any stipulations about size or ritual. Lesley College students universally disapproved of lying in state. The other groups did not express an opinion on this point.

Most Memorable Image

Although the photographic juxtaposition of photographs from *Gramp* (Figures 114, 64) was the image chosen most often as most memorable by all populations, there was a great deal of variation in the selection of other images. Among the junior and senior high school students, the images and artifacts from popular culture and those depicting literal or symbolic visions of the afterlife were popular. Lesley College students frequently selected images of the afterlife. The medical students were extremely varied in their selections but tended to gravitate toward more realistic or photographic portrayals of death. Not surprisingly, the same was true for nurses who also work in a scientific environment, a hospital setting. Memorable for the nurses were *The Death of Socrates* (Figure 5), the photographs of palliative care patients and families (Figures 75, 81, 109–113), and the slides dealing with existential aloneness and communication among family members (Figures 10, 92, 95). The gamut of choice was widest among the hospice volunteers, from the communication images or lack of it between family members at the deathbed to the artifacts from popular culture.

NOTES

1. Quote modified from Kazantzakis, N. (1952). *Zorba the Greek* (p. 269). New York: Simon and Schuster.

4

Broadening the Perspective

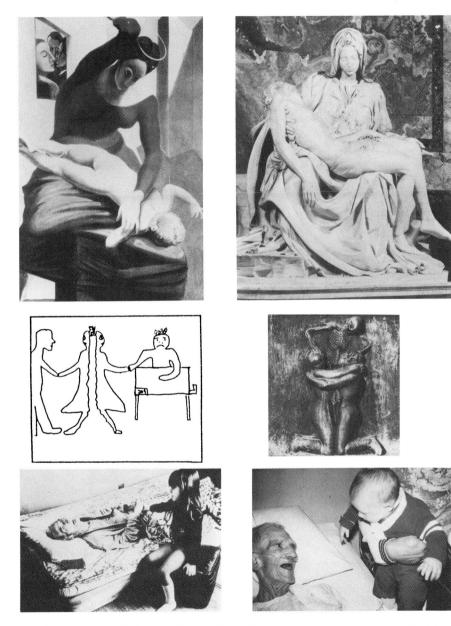

In its myriad forms death through art opens our eyes to limitless possibilities.

Juxtaposition of Figure 71 with Figure 38, Figure 116 with Figure 1, and Figure 107 with Figure 113.

Chapter 4

Broadening the Perspective

In both teaching and counseling, I try to encourage a broader appreciation of the experience of death. The arts enable us to probe the human condition in language that is symbolic rather than literal, suggestive rather than didactic. As such, they are the best kind of teacher. Through metaphor the arts challenge, instruct, and support us in our endeavor to endure another's suffering and to understand our own.

The beauty of the arts is that they can be adapted to the needs of any audience, and that they allow astute discussion leaders or therapists to linger over pressing concerns. Since the arts speak to everyone regardless of age, sex, socioeconomic status, or intellectual sophistication, they are universally embracing and have the potential to evoke uncommonly profound reactions from audiences of all types. In short, the arts are a superb means of leading audiences to become more sensitive observers of and participants in the experiences of life that are common to us all.

Vital to the presentations—at least at some time in a group meeting—is that the images be viewed in double-slide or multiple format. Juxtapositions of pairs of visual images or visual and literary images allow for a multiplicity of viewpoints and serve to heighten the connectedness of the senses, particularly of sight and sound. In addition, forced juxtaposition of apparently incongruous images often has the effect of breaking down emotional barriers, biases, or preconceptions that may block spontaneous responses. Even abstract images paired with more concrete forms have a way of loosening emotional restraints, thereby giving way to a previously untapped or unexpressed wealth of insight.

Despite preconceived notions about the nature of grief and expectations of vast differences in the populations I have studied, I have discovered several truths:

That death, like birth, is an archetypically communal experience with universally shared emotions, fears, hopes, and pains—an event that ironically has *not* changed despite advanced technology and sophisticated medical care;

That in seeking to improve our own professional abilities to deal with death and dying, healthcare workers, therapists, and educators can continue to address their own previously unacknowledged grief and may even find solace in its revival or in becoming reacquainted with it;

That although there is no end to death, there can be an evolution or "transformation" of grief;

That art, presented in a sensitive, nonthreatening format with a carefully directed focus, can evoke deeply personal understanding and can provide a sort of emotional vaccination that induces protection and a sense of empowerment, community, and humaneness;

That "doing unto others what one might wish for oneself" provides both balm and healing in the death experience and that the arts can serve as valuable adjunct to the human hand extended in consolation (Figure 172).

Figure 172. *Woman Reaching Out her Hand to Death* (1934), Kathe Kollwitz. Lithograph, 46 × 39.5. National Gallery of Art. Washington, DC, Rosenwald Collection.

FACING DEATH: GUIDELINES FOR USING THE ARTS

Although it is easy to acknowledge that art complements teaching, counseling, or bereavement work, it is no simple task to overcome the barriers that art often erects. Yet, one does not need an advanced degree in art history or literary analysis to be able to use the arts successfully. All that is necessary is an openness to observation and a sensitivity to the myriad interpretations that can emerge when the world of the arts is approached.

I offer some guidelines in response to the following questions that so often arise in the training workshops:

How can I use the arts in my role as social worker, teacher, counselor?

How do I analyze a work of art? Is there a formula?

How can I "unblock" inhibition or resistance to art (my own included)?

What can I do to alleviate burnout (for my staff, colleagues, and myself)?

What if slide projection isn't feasible?

How are the arts applicable to counseling techniques?

In what other arenas have you found the arts useful?

How can I involve participants more in the presentation?

On using the arts

First, become comfortable with art. If you like paintings or photographs, begin there. Choose images that evoke a deep emotional response or reaction in yourself. They are bound to touch others. Consciously keep a record of such reactions and try to apply them to real-life situations.

Expand your horizons. Select some literary art to accompany your images. Don't restrict yourself to poetry and fiction—the newsstand, the greeting card store, even city-street graffiti are full of provocative and often blatantly well-put sentiments.

Consider ways to incorporate the performing arts such as music, dance, drama, film, and opera into your presentations. Compare similar themes in different art works (e.g., *Camille* in painting, film, and opera, or Camille and the Sleeping Beauty fairy tale). Juxtapose the incongruous: Socrates in David's *The Death of Socrates* (Figure 5) and black dancer Dudley Williams in "I Wanna Be Ready." Both Socrates and Williams are "on their toes," so to speak, en route to the afterlife. The lyrics of the gospel song and the choreography have Williams dressing to meet his maker. The discussion can be religious, moral, political, aesthetic, or whatever the atmosphere requires.

Two sensitively executed film/video pieces document the everyday moments of despair and dignity in the lives of ordinary (but truly *extraordinary*) people coping with terminal illness. The 28-minute film *Walk Me to the Water* chronicles the experiences of three terminally ill cancer patients dying at home. I am particularly moved by the 17-minute segment about Marion, who is cared for by her daughter, son-in-law, and grandson. More frighteningly stark is the 27-minute *So Sad, So Sorry, So What*. Our own prejudices, moral values, and assumptions are exposed by JoAnne, a young single mother, recovering addict, and prison inmate who through her own words and haunting songs draws us into the painful past and uncertain future of her AIDS diagnosis. Used together, both films show the paradoxical fear and confusion, the possibilities for individual failure and growth, and the weakening and strengthening of family bonds that can accompany these distresses.

Literary companion pieces to these visual portraits include the short stores *Tell Me A Riddle* by Tillie Olsen and *The Death of Ivan Ilyich* by Tolstoy. Olsen's dying grandmother and Marion provide fertile ground for discussing family relationships, especially those between mother and child, grandmother and grandchild. Parallel moments of miscommunication, anguish, and solace abound in the father-son, mother-son relationships of *The Death of Ivan Ilyich* and *So Sad, So Sorry, So What*. Viewed together, all four works challenge every principle of family dynamics and also invite discussion about the deficiencies of our healthcare system.

The films are available through the following distributors: (1) *So Sad, So Sorry, So What*, Jan Gillooly, b/w 27 mins. Fanlight Productions, 47 Halifax St., Boston, MA 02130; (2) *Walk Me to the Water*, John Seakwood, b/w 28 mins. Walk Me to the Water, Box 258 Bird Rd., New Lebanon, NY 12125.

Figure 5. (See page 15).

On approaching painting analysis

Project on the screen or distribute a single image for analysis. The following questions can be modified and applied to any work of art:

From the Viewer's Perspective

What do you see?
What is the subject of the work?
What do you think is going on in the picture (poem, cartoon)?
Identify the characters. What are the relationships between or among them?
What are the background details?
What colors and compositional elements are used: color, line, shading? How and why?
What is odd? Missing? Distorted? What stands out?

Applied to *The Death of Socrates*, the following *specific* questions expand the analysis:

Who is the man seated at center?
Who are the other figures around him? In the hallway? Going up the stairs?

Who is the old man at the foot of the bed facing in the other direction?
What is in the cup and who is the man holding it? Why is he, too, turned away?
What is the significance of the hand pointing upward?
Where is this scene taking place?
What is the source of light?
What is the significance of the objects on the floor (chain and scroll)?
Why does the central figure have a head that seems older than his body?

From the Artist's Perspective

Although discussion about artists' intentions are limited to conjecture, it might be fruitful to ask:

Why was the picture painted? Was it commissioned? Was it a recording of a powerful memory? Was it intended to be a memorial? An exercise?
Is the artist making a social or political statement? Is the intention to portray a psychological, spiritual, or interior reality?

Even more specifically:

What is the significance of the title?
The artist has selected a particular constellation of images to tell a story. What story is he trying to tell?
Why do you think the artist has positioned or portrayed the figures this way?
What kinds of feelings and thoughts are being conveyed through the positioning of figures, other objects or elements, use of composition and light, gestures, clothing, color?
What are the historical, social, and autobiographic contexts and how do they help you uncover the artist's intention?

In this example, the title identifies David's *The Death of Socrates*:

Why is David painting this scene—which occurred in ancient Greece—at the time of the French Revolution?
Why has he employed another anachronism, portraying Plato as an old man?

Why has he banished the women to the background? Is the implication
that he is sparing his wife? That such a scene is too difficult for her
and the women?

Why is the student touching Socrates's knee? Is David suggesting that
Socrates is using his death to teach his students?

Historical details, especially applied to older works, can lend additional shading and color. Get to know the "old masters" that you employ.
Read about their history. For example, David painted *The Death of Socrates*
at a time when the old order in France was being overthrown. What does
this fact add to the details of the painting? "Discourse is the greatest good
of mankind: and a life unexamined is a life unlived," wrote Socrates. How
might Socrates's own words be applied?

From the Emotional Perspective

Probe the feelings of your audience through the following questions:

What are you experiencing? (e.g., boredom, anger, amusement, sadness?)
How does the painting make you feel? (e.g., ill, sad, happy, worried,
ashamed?)

David's painting, for most groups, seems to have more cerebral than
emotional impact. To explore your audience's feelings, you may want to
contrast this painting with pieces that have more visceral appeal. Choose
a poetic or lyric piece, either the one from *The Woman Said Yes*, in which
she mentions the "cannonball" in her stomach (Figure 83) or the passage
from *The Shadow Box* describing the smells, the "shits and vomits" of advanced cancer (Figure 69), applicable clearly to AIDS.

From the Symbolic Perspective

Approach the concerns of your specific audience—medical students,
nurses, social workers, volunteers. Focus the discussion on transforming
values and developing new insights.

How does this work change your view of caring for or interacting with
seriously ill persons?
How can these insights be employed in our personal and professional
lives?

How does this work prompt us to look at our own moral values and assumptions?

Applied to David's painting, the following questions could be posed.

Why are the scrolls on the floor? Is the suggestion that the writing of philosophy is not as important as living the life of moral action? Is the role of the doer more important than the one describing it?

Is Socrates the supreme example of putting one's beliefs into action and taking the risks for them?

Compare the young physician caring for Mr. Kahn who wanted to be unhooked from the machines and "die like a mensch" ("Dying in Academe"): are there conflicts between what we hold abstractly and how we act in practice? If we believe in the living will, how do we translate this belief into action?

Is David's painting more about choice and self-respect than about death? Is Socrates choosing to live by his convictions? The price happens to be death. Is he questioning the established order? Is willing to die for a higher truth a religious or philosophical issue?

On "unblocking" inhibition and resistance to art

Have your audience write a scenario about a specific image or create one in the context of their role as nurses, volunteers, family members. For example, offer Munch's *Death Agony* (Figure 95) and ask them to create a narrative about the circumstances of the picture, the figures depicted, and how they might modify the scene to the effect of a good death for the dying person or a more satisfactory resolution for the family members. Is a healthcare professional present? Exactly where does he or she belong?

● ● ●

Present a detail from a painting or a captionless cartoon and have group members fill in the background or provide the caption.

Detail

Figure 176. *AIDS Patient* (1989), Luis Cruz Azaceta. Acryllic on canvas, 48 × 36. Courtesy Frumkin/Adams Gallery, New York.

Example I: Detail from Luis Cruz Azaceta's Painting (Figure 11)

Various respondents have placed family around the bedside, pulled the plug, softened the scene by covering the harsh lightbulb, placed themselves holding his hand, piped in music, included his dog. A few of the more evocative negative responses are reproduced below; they suggest anonymity and loneliness, callous healthcare professionals, fear of contagion (Figures 173–175).

Figure 173.

Figure 174.

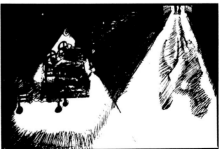

Figures 173–175. Images from students and healthcare professionals, workshop. (1990). "AIDS: Perspectives for Caregivers." University of Massachusetts Medical School, Worcester, MA. Bertman Collection.

Figure 175.

After sharing the group's responses, discuss the detail in its intended context (Figure 176). What is being said by having the protagonist isolated among a sea of statistics?

Example II: Phillips Cartoon of Elderly Couple in Hospital Bed (Figure 88)

What a way to go!

O.K. Who gets the enema?

So who called for you?

We lived together. We'll die together.

• • •

We are constantly being bombarded by visual messages. With a daily newspaper, some magazines, scissors, rubber cement, and magic markers, the educator and counselor have excellent resources for those who are self-conscious about their ability to render "correct" images to complete the initial assignment. Participants who choose not to draw an image can "construct" a multimedia one, altering and writing new titles for existing images at will with the markers. Collages made of many brightly colored pictures cut from magazines offer even wider possibilities for multiple layers of personal meaning (Figures 177 and 178).

Figure 177.

Figure 178.

Figures 177 and 178.   Collages from medical students. University of Massachusetts Medical School, class of 1993.

Figures 177 and 178 are images created by medical students. They suggest the multifaceted challenge posed by human dissection and the inevitable intertwining of their own lives with those of their cadavers and future patients.

• • •

Use a simple work of art like Jill Lion's sculpture (Figure 179) to establish the mood for a discussion. Invite participants to imitate the pose in the sculpture. When they are positioned, solicit comments about how

Figure 179. *Waiting for the Diagnosis*, retitled *Terror* (1989), Jill Lion. Limestone, 8 × 8 × 18. Photograph by Gary Garrison. Permission of the artist.

they are feeling, what they are thinking. Read to them an evocative literary image, like Alice Walker's "Medicine" (Figure 91) or Emily Dickinson's "After Great Pain a Formal Feeling Comes." Note: This technique will not work well in highly inhibited or resistant groups.

• • •

Have group members select a passage from a story or poem to illustrate, amplify, or contradict. One college student chose a passage from the assigned story "Tell Me A Riddle." Her watercolor does more than simply illustrate a passage from Tillie Olsen's text. In our discussion of the piece, we realized we had seen death portrayed in many ways: as the deceiver, the seducer, the father figure, and equalizer, but never as the one grieving (Figure 180).

> "The cards fell from his fingers. Without warning, the bereavement and betrayal he had sheltered—compounded through the years—hidden even from himself—revealed itself ... and with it the monstrous shapes of what had actually happened in the century."

Figure 180. Student image. "Death Crying." Equinox Collection.

On alleviating burnout

The double-slide or double-easel technique is an excellent way to prevent burnout for the teacher or counselor accustomed to constantly showing the same images together. Reshuffling the images forces us to reenter the dialogue anew, to view these "old friends" from yet another perspective.

Consider Munch's *Death Agony* (Figure 95) juxtaposed against:

Figure 95. (See page 85).

Figure 95. (See page 85).

Figure 181   Rembrandt. This interpretation places the dying person at center stage, rather than the bereaved, and demonstrates tranquil unity and the "teaching moment" of the deathbed scene.

Figure 181.   *Jacob Blessing Sons of Joseph* (1656), Harmenszoon van Rijn Rembrandt. Oil on canvas. Staatliche Kunstsammlungen Kassel, Gemaldegalerie Alte Meister.

Figure 95. (See page 85).

Figure 182   Benny Allen. This death vigil is similar to Munch's portrayal in that community support is ironically offered by individuals lost in private thoughts or grief.

Figure 182.   *The Wait* (1974), Benny Andrews. 18 × 12³/4. Reprinted in *Between the Lines* (1978). Pella Publishing Company, New York. Courtesy of the artist.

Figure 95. (See page 85).

Figure 183   Sir Luke Fildes. This painting emphasizes the comforting presence of the physician in the most tragic of all deaths—that of a child.

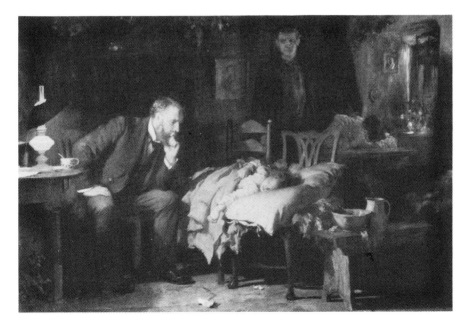

Figure 183.   *Physician Watching Over a Sick Child* (1891), Sir Luke Fildes. New York Academy of Medicine Library, New York.

Reshuffle the images and consider other juxtapositions:

View Beckmann's *Large Death Scene* (Figure 10) juxtaposed with the quotation from *The Shadow Box* (Figure 69); anger can be viewed as positive, as part of the embrace of love.

Figure 10. (See page 19).

You can wipe up the mucous and the blood and the piss and excrement. You can burn the sheets and boil his clothes, but it's still there. You can smell it on him.

You can smell it on me. It gets into your blood ... you can taste it on him, you can swallow it and feel it inside your belly like a sewer.

You wake up at night and you shake and you spit. You try to vomit it out of you. Inside every word, every move, every day, every touch, every night, it lies down with you and gets in between you. It's sick and putrid and soft and rotten and it is killing me.

Contrast the ideal and the real in the photograph of Camille's death (Figure 9) with that of Gramp toileting (Figure 78).

Figure 9. (See page 18).

Figure 78. (See page 65).

Juxtapose Woody Allen's attitude toward dying (Figure 17) with Ivan Ilyich's death scene (Figure 98); secular versus spiritual.

> **... The fear that there may be no afterlife—a depressing thought, particularly for those who have bothered to shave; also, there is a fear that there *is* an afterlife but no one will know where it is being held.**

His hand fell on the boy's head, and the boy caught it, pressed it to his lips and began to cry. . . . He opened his eyes, looked at his son and felt sorry for him.

In place of death there was light . . . "So that's what it is! . . . What joy!" . . . "Death is finished . . . it is no more!" He drew in a breath, stopped in the middle of a sigh, stretched out, and died.

• • •

Professional burnout is another area that the arts can address naturally. The simple act of stepping back from day to day reality into the abstract world of art and literature can be rejuvenating. Such a retreat can take the form of 15 minutes in a quiet room with a "Walkman" and your favorite art book, a leisurely stroll through a familiar museum, or even a visit to a theater or movie. Let the arts provide the catharsis necessary to freshen your perspective and bolster your emotional reserves.

On alternatives to slide projection

Though the presentation discussed in Chapter 2 was composed of photographic slides, the development of modern photocopying equipment offers an inexpensive means to reproduce art for classroom purposes. The teacher should investigate the many firms that now offer color photocopies both for reproducing art works from books and student drawings. Other machines can create transparencies for overhead projectors from color slides as well. Please make every effort to respect copyright restrictions.

• • •

The recent popularity of video technology has made it a regular presence in our classrooms, hospitals, and volunteer centers. Full-length videos abound on a variety of topics. The creative "editor" however, can develop a series of video vignettes to address any of the subjects suggested in this book.

Example: On Saying Goodbye

Select filmed versions of parting or death sequences from feature-length films. Cue the films to an appropriate starting point or intercut scenes on a separate tape. Ask your audience to discuss the verbal and nonverbal language employed in both the dying and those in attendance. When appropriate, solicit alternative phrasings and positioning. Suggested films include: *Terms of Endearment, Cocoon, Gone with the Wind, Wuthering Heights, Steel Magnolias, Longtime Companions.* Or make use of the legitimate theater and professional or college performances: *The Normal Heart, The Shadow Box, Les Miserables, The Rink, Falsettoland.* If time permits, many feature length films or plays in their entirety offer marvelous resources for the trajectory from diagnosis through death and bereavement: *Ikiru, Terms of Endearment, Whose Life is it, Anyway?, Always, Ghost.*

On applying the arts to counseling and communication skills

Before or at the beginning of the meeting, choose an image or have group members individually select one image for consideration. Ask each one to write a scenario about the image from the point of view of his or her role as nurse, volunteer, family member. In pairs or groups of three or four, invite members to share their scenarios. Choose one for a more in-depth analysis. In the large group setting, role play and utilize the image psychodramatically:

Set the scene, approximate as much as possible the artist's setting to the details of placing objects as pictures or shadows.

Position yourself (or reverse roles) with/as a character in the scenario and
begin a dialogue.

Let various members of the group serve as the protagonist's "double" or
alter ego. When conversation lags, others can step in to replace characters or other elements in the scene.

Be sure to "debrief" group members in the ensuing discussion.

Munch's graphic *Compassion* (Figure 90) is an excellent example. The
figure with her hands hiding her face might be a person with AIDS or
cancer or a daughter who has expressed guilt for not having been present
when her mother died. The other figure could be a visiting nurse or volunteer. The black shape in these instances would be the spectre of HIV or
cancer personified (the person's fears and concerns) or the dead mother.
The visiting nurse or volunteer begins and responds, in role, to the subsequent dialogue.

Figure 90. (See page 75).

What generally emerges from an exercise of this type is an active
portrayal of the discomfort of the moment. In addition, the group learns
to generate alternative means for handling "worst-case" scenarios as unmentionable feelings become articulated.

Other arenas for employing the arts

Other subjects that may be covered using the same techniques include understanding problems that accompany physical and neurological disabilities of all kinds, deformities from burn accidents and surgery, drug abuse, homelessness, and any other loss or death we try to minimize, avoid, or deny.

One of the populations that our culture tends to dismiss is the elderly infirm. In this exercise, let the theme be "facing aging" or "facing disability." The arts provide a marvelous entrée into these worlds. As we have seen in the instances of deathbed scenes, the arts grant us permission to stare without shame at the physically, mentally, and spiritually impaired. We do not have to avert our eyes. The work of art invites close inspection and takes responsibility for propriety, all the while keeping us focused on larger questions of human decency. The artist or writer leads us beyond the physical, beyond even the psychological, to wander through existential and humanistic realms (Figures 184, 185).

For the visually impaired, the same subject matter can be covered through song, either performed live or tape-recorded. A sing-a-long might

Figure 184.   *An Old Man and His Grandson* (1480), Dr. Ghirlandaio. The Louvre, Paris.

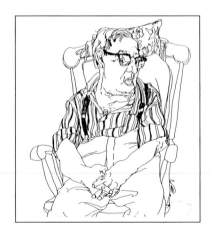

Figure 185.   Michael Jacques (1980). "Northfield Convalescent." *Images of Age.* ABT Books, Cambridge, MA. Permission of the artist.

be a refreshing change of pace for elderly groups or for any of us. Some suggestions for audio cuts include: "Old Friends," Paul Simon; "I'd Rather Be Dead," Harry Nilson; "When You Are Old And Gray," Tom Lehrer; "Old Folks," Mort Shuman and Eric Blau; "Hello in There," John Prine; "When I'm Sixty-Four," John Lennon and Paul McCartney; "Old Man," Randy Newman; "Too Old To Work," Joe Glazer; "Grandma's Battlecry," Irene Paul; "The Activity Room," Ruth Pelem; "When I Grow Too Old To Dream," Oscar Hammerstein, II, Sigmund Romberg.

• • •

Despite the fact that AIDS is, like cancer, a chronic and terminal illness, AIDS is a disease that has evoked more fear, misunderstanding, superstition, and anger than any other medical problem in the 20th century. Judging by the increase in cases projected by our health statisticians, every healthcare provider and counselor desperately needs to confront his or her feelings about this modern "plague" so that dispassionate, objective help can be offered when meeting people with HIV and AIDS.

First, we are shocked that a communicable disease has escaped the tight knot of vaccination and protection we have developed in a century that has seen the eradication of smallpox, measles, polio, and venereal disease and cures for tuberculosis. Second, in a nation that has learned to keep its elderly alive longer and longer, AIDS shocks us because it kills young people, children, and even those not yet born.

An excellent way to start an arts project is to collect AIDS posters. Begin with your local health department or AIDS Action Committee. What are the messages? What images are used, and how are they handled? Comment on the images and intention (prevention, empathy, political statement). What makes a particular image successful? Have participants devise posters of their own (Figure 186).

Figure 186.   Participant's AIDS poster. Bertman Collection.

To initiate discussion, have your group look at AIDS memorials that have already been created—the AIDS Quilt, the walk-a-thon "From All Walks of Life," and *Epitaphs for the Living: Words and Images in the Time of AIDS*, a collection of photographs inscribed in most cases by the subjects in their own handwriting. Photographer Billy Howard wanted his subjects' own voices to be heard. Some used their space to react to their pain and treatment; they did so with rage, humor, hope, even affirmation. Some used their space to say goodbye. The image of a tiny baby girl alone in a hospital room is signed with her handprint. The viewer-reader almost unconsciously develops a greater understanding of the tragic ramifications of this medical-cultural monster and a sympathetic appreciation for the uniqueness of the lives it has so mercilessly spent (Figures 187, 188).

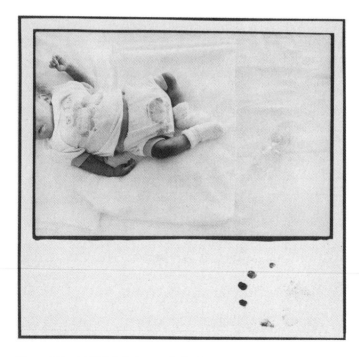

Figure 188. "AIDS Baby." *Epitaphs for the Living:Words and Images in the Time of AIDS* (1989). Photographs by Billy Howard. Southern Methodist University Press, Dallas.

Figure 187. "Pat and Ron." *Epitaphs for the Living: Words and Images in the Time of AIDS* (1989). Photographs by Billy Howard. Southern Methodist University Press, Dallas.

On involving participants more in the presentation

The images of death drawn by many participants in anticipation of the death and dying workshop are often beautiful and striking original creations that merit incorporation into future slide presentations. Many reveal an almost archetypal understanding of the death experience and consequently reflect a shared vision with the "great masters." It is also interesting to note the universality of themes that are selected, and by extension, the commonality of the experience of death. It is both comforting and enlightening to witness this age-old sharing.

Accordingly, it might be interesting and provocative to prepare new double-slide presentations in which images created by previous audiences play a more significant role. These could be effectively employed in juxtaposition with the images regularly used or with other participants' drawings that share a similar theme. The possibilities are virtually limitless.

The following are four examples of how the teacher, counselor, or group leader can use student, patient, or group members' works. It is preferable to use color reproductions, since color images are generally more evocative, and one can also address choice of color. Each of these illustrations could serve very well in juxtaposition with many of the images from the double-slide presentation.

Example I: Facing Death

I'm afraid of needles.
I'm tired of rubber sheets and tubes.
I'm tired of faces that I don't know
and now I think that death is starting.
Death starts like a dream,
full of objects and my sister's laughter.
We are young and we are walking
and picking wild blueberries
all the way to Damariscotta.

Oh Susan, she cried,
you've stained your new waist
Sweet taste —
and the sweet blue running out
All the way to Damariscotta.
What are you doing? Leave me alone!
Can't you see I'm dreaming?
In a dream you are never eighty.

Figure 189. "Old." Anne Sexton. From *All My Pretty Ones*. Copyright 1962 by Anne Sexton. Reprinted by permission of Houghton Mifflin Company, Boston.

Figure 10. (See page 19).

Figure 132. (See page 114).

With the exception of the spectators in the Beckmann painting, both illustrations show a remarkable similarity of line, and contrast nicely in the historical periods they evoke. The poetry suggests the peacefulness of dreaming or death, and the group might discuss whether the subjects are dying or dead, the setting, and who else is in attendance.

Example II: Three Evocations

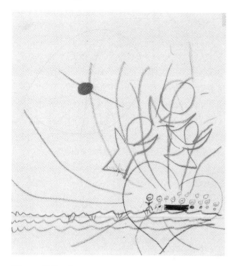

Figure 130. (See page 113).

Figure 31. (See page 23).

Figure 170. (See page 149).

These are examples of illustrations that evoke the concept of afterlife with beneficient spirits looking down over the mourners after death. Note the interesting relationships that endure between the living and the dead, and the suggestion that the dead warm the earth like sunshine or love. All three illustrations suggest grief work accomplished through art.

Example III: Three Medical Students and a Poet

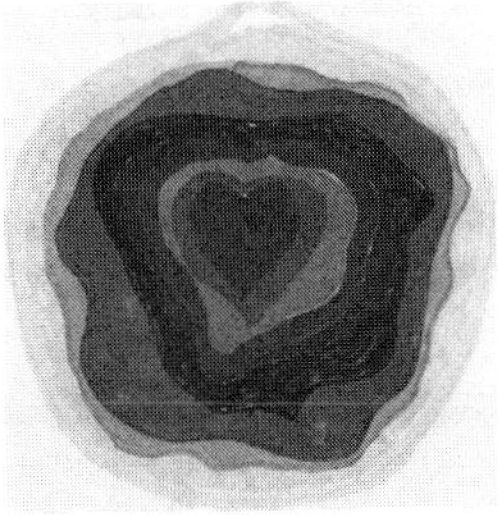

I am not dead, I have only become inhuman:
That is to say,
Undressed myself of laughable prides and infirmities,
But not as a man
Undresses to creep into bed, but like an athlete
Stripping for the race.
The delicate ravel of nerves that made me a measurer
Of certain fictions
Called good and evil; that made me contract with pain
And expand with pleasure;
Fussily adjusted like a little electroscope:
That's gone, it is true;
(I never miss it; if the universe does,
How easily replaced!)
But all the rest is heightened, widened, set free.
I admired the beauty
While I was human. Now I am part of the beauty.
I wander in the air,
Being mostly gas and water, and flow in the ocean;
Touch you and Asia
At the same moment; have a hand in the sunrises
And the glow of this grass.
I left the light precipitate of ashes to earth
For a love-token.

Figure 159. (See page 129).

Figure 158. (See page 128).

Figure 162. (See page 130).

Figure 190. "Inscription for a Gravestone." Robinson Jeffers.
(1931). Copyright 1931 by Random House, Inc., and renewed
1959 by Robinson Jeffers. Reprinted from *Selected Poetry of
Robinson Jeffers,* by permission of Random House, Inc.

These three illustrations reveal a theme that is common to many images created by medical students: the *layering* of the body, at the core of
which lies the heart. Note the similarity in the use of color and particularly the role played by the color *grey.* Medical students frequently view
the dissection experience—and consequently the life-death experience—
as a journey through many levels of understanding. The Jeffers poem
echoes the notion of layering, and treats the subject matter in appropri-
ately scientific language, tone, and "coloration."

Example IV: Visions of Death

Figure 131. (See page 113).

Figure 122. (See page 110).

Figure 126. (See page 112).

I shall not be imprisoned in that grave where you are to bury my body. I shall be diffused in great nature, in the soil, in the air, in the sunshine, in the hearts of those who love me.

Figure 40. (See page 37).

These three Lesley college students' images reveal a refreshing variation of attitudes toward death. Each is striking in its thematic treatment
and use of color. The first suggests death as inextricably linked to birth
and life. Note the central image of a heart connected to a bleeding umbilical cord, which appears to "water the earth," producing blood-red fruit.
The delicate brushstrokes of the second illustration have created a peaceful dove in flight. Its wings are in harmony with the brightly colored
backdrop, which suggests life. Death in this interpretation is not static and
bleak but active and vivid. In the third image, death is portrayed as a
movement from the greenness of life to the blackness of burial. The illustration suggests, however, that the survivors, through memory, are able to
keep a portion of the deceased out of the grave (i.e., though the body may
die, the spirit remains alive in those who survive).

FACING DEATH: SOME COUNSELING GUIDELINES

The following guidelines were developed as a result of the need perceived in these death and dying seminars for a concrete, "take-home"
message that could be useful to any group. The guidelines are not intended alone for healthcare workers or individuals involved in grief counseling. Anyone may serve in the role of comforter for family members,
friends, and others in need.

The counselor's own feelings

The loss of a loved person is one of the most intensely painful experiences any human being can suffer. Not only is it painful to experience; it is
also painful to witness. We want to be helpful, but instead we may experience feelings of frustration, anger, and impotence. Counseling or peer
assistance in a situation of grief can trigger our own sense of vulnerability
and awareness of our own losses, real or potential. Reflection on our own
losses and how we coped with them is an excellent avenue to the empa-
thetic sharing of other people's grief.

What do I say?

Say what you feel. Death has a way of sealing people off, making them feel totally isolated. Sharing feelings—*real* feelings—reestablishes connection. If you feel sorry, angry, or bewildered, say so. Tears are also a powerful way to demonstrate a common humanity. Crying together is a beautiful way to share sadness. If crying is not comfortable, encouraging others to vent emotions and feelings is another source of help: "Go ahead and cry (or scream)—it's all right." Admitting you *don't* know what to say is O.K. Your presence speaks louder than words.

Part of dealing with the sense of being cut off—for both the one dying and the one bereaved—is acknowledging that though a vital part of life has changed dramatically, all relationships (with friends, even with you, perhaps) have not. Furthermore, survivors can learn to continue a relationship with the memory of the deceased after the sadness, anger, fear, and bitterness have been addressed, and to draw from it solace and support. For as Robert Anderson tells us in *I Never Sang for My Father*, "Death ends a life, but not a relationship . . . ."

What about the stage theories?

Most people are aware of Elizabeth Kubler-Ross's five stages of grief: denial, anger, bargaining, depression, acceptance. Kubler-Ross did not intend this to be a cookbook formula. Other researchers have postulated different "stage" constructs. Cancers can be "staged"; grief cannot. What is helpful about such theories is that they give us a sense of the emotional roller coaster experienced by persons who are grieving. Denial is, at times, as adaptive a coping mechanism as is humor. In general, there appear to be three "phases":

Denial, shock and protest;
Disorganization, despair (also phrased as a hope/despair cycle or emotional suffering);
Reintegration, repatterning, transformation, or adaption.

Although it is important to recognize the emotional variability that a dying or bereaved person experiences, it is equally important to realize that interventions are appropriate and effective at any phase of grieving.

How do I help someone grieve?

Grieving is active. It is *work*. It requires remembering repetitively experiences shared with the dead person, over a long period of time; *talking about* and *expressing* the mixed emotional ties—particularly the anger, remorse, and sadness, perhaps, even relief—until the devastating potency of the loss is neutralized.

The most important balm a counselor can offer is presence and concern. *You are facilitating the grieving process by being there*: by listening, nonjudgmentally, and be reassuring the bereaved persons that they are not "going crazy." You can affirm that the acute pain they are experiencing is grief in process, and that it will not last forever.

1. Encourage the saying of goodbyes at the bedside, before death, whenever possible.
2. Encourage active participation in the care of the person dying, in being present at the moment of death, and even in preparing the body for burial. There is great solace in knowing "I was there and I did all that I could."
3. Encourage involvement with the mourning rituals of funeral, eulogy, celebration, and memorial services. Such rites provide outlets for the expression of sorrow and help delineate the grieving process. Viewing the dead body helps one accept the fact of death. Unveilings and anniversary rites also mark the progress of grief.
4. Listen, nonjudgmentally, realizing, as Samuel Coleridge's Ancient Mariner reminds us, that the albatross of grief falls off with retelling the story. Encourage reminiscences, the painful as well as the positive, and expression of the hostile, angry, and negative feelings that seem so incompatible with the genuine love for the dying or dead person. Again, offer reassurance that such ambivalence is normal.
5. Monitor your own feelings. You are not immune to sadness, anxiety, or the need to express personal concern. Your reactions are conditioned by your own experiences with earlier losses and by your ability to handle hostile reactions from those you are counseling: friend, patient, client, student, or family member.
6. Be informed about self-help support groups such as "Candlelighters," "Living with Cancer," "Sibs with Cancer," "People with

AIDS," "Widow-to-Widow" and bereavement programs sponsored by churches, hospitals, hospices, and civic organizations in
your community. Such groups assist in answering practical questions, in understanding feelings, in providing networks, and in en-
abling participants to reach out to others as they gain mastery in
their own personal experiences.

7. Know when referral is necessary. You are in a good position to
detect unresolved and complicated grief and pathological mourning and, when you suspect a severe problem, you should enlist
additional psychotherapeutic help.

Grief is not a disease. It is love not wanting to let go. It can be likened
to a "blow" or a cut in which the wound gradually heals. For a while, one
is acutely vulnerable, physically and emotionally. Though grief can be
temporarily disabling, working through it ultimately brings strength.
Colin Murray Parkes sums it up nicely in his book, *Bereavement*, reminding
us just as broken bones may knit together more strongly, so the experience
of grieving can strengthen or mature those who have previously been
shielded from misfortune: "The pain of grief is just as much a part of life
as the joy of love; it is, perhaps, the price we pay for love, the cost of
commitment. To ignore this fact . . . is to put on emotional blinders which
leave us unprepared for the losses that will inevitably occur in our own
lives and unprepared to help others to cope with the losses in theirs."

• • •

The arts, then, can provide an invaluable entrée into the diversity of
the universal experiences of death, dying, grief, and loss. The personal
value of controlled, enlightened introspection notwithstanding, the methods detailed here, hopefully serve still another purpose. They help to re-
store a measure of humanity to today's frighteningly impersonal medical-
industrial complex. By focusing attention on the individual—by seeking
to establish or reestablish connections between our emotional and professional personae, we can help to smooth the rough terrain of intention and
desire that often lies between patient and provider, patient and family, and

individual and psyche. With unwavering attention to the universality of experience and the simple truth expressed by art through the ages, we can bolster our humanity not simply through the obvious benefits we derive from a good life but from the strength and consolation we gain through acknowledging a good death.

• • •

"Death is not the enemy, Doctor. Inhumanity is."

Bibliography and Additional Reading

Allen, W. (1987). *Getting even.* New York: Random House.
Allen, W. (1987). *Hannah and her sisters.* New York: Random House.
Anthony, S. (1987). *The discovery of death in childhood and after.* New York: Random House.
Aries, P. (1974). *Western attitudes toward death.* Baltimore, MD: The Johns Hopkins University Press.
Arras, J., & Hunt, R. (1983). *Ethical issues in modern medicine.* Palo Alto, CA: Mayfield Publishing Company.
Becker, E. (1973). *The denial of death.* New York: The Free Press.
Benoliel, J. Q. (1982). *Death education for the health professional.* Washington: Hemisphere Publishing.
Bertman, S. L. (1974). Death education in the face of a taboo. In E. Grollman (Ed.). *Concerning death: A practical guide for the living.* Boston, MA: Beacon.
Bertman, S. L. (1979, 1985). The arts: A source of comfort and insight for children who are learning about death. In R. Kalish (Ed.). *The final transition.* Farmingdale, NY: Baywood Publishing.
Bertman, S. L., Greene, H., & Wyatt, C. (1982). Humanistic health care in a hospice/palliative care setting. In J. Benoliel (Ed.). *Death education for the health care professional.* New York: McGraw-Hill.
Bertman, S. L. (1980). Lingering terminal illness and the family: Insights from literature. *Journal of Family Process* 19, 341–348.
Bertman, S. L. (1983). Bearing the unbearable: From loss, the gain. *Health values: Achieving high level wellness.* 7(1) 24–32.
Bertman, S. L. (1984). Helping children cope with death. In J. Hansen & T. Franz (Eds.). *Death and grief in the family.* The Family Therapy Collections. Rockville, MD: Aspen Systems Corp.
Bertman, S. L. (1989). Aging grace: Treatments of the aged in the arts. *Death Studies* 13, 517–535.
Bertman, S. L. In press. Death education: The classroom and living room revisited. In R. Stevenson (Ed.). *Curing death ignorance: Death education in the school.* New York: Haworth.
Bertman, S. L., & Krant, M. J. (1977). To know of suffering and the teaching of empathy. *Social Science and Medicine* 11, 639–644.
Bertman, S. L., & Marks, S. J. Jr. (1989). The dissection experience as a laboratory for self-discovery about death and dying: Another side of clinical anatomy. *Clinical Anatomy* 2, 103–113.
Bertman, S. L., & Marks, S. C., Jr. (1985). Humanities in medical education: Rationale and resources for the dissection laboratory. *Medical Education* 19, 374–381.
Bertman, S. L., Sumpter, H., & Freene, H. (1991). Bereavement and grief. In H. Greene (Ed.). *Introduction to clinical medicine.* Philadelphia: B. C. Decker.
Bertman, S. L., Wertheimer, M. D., & Wheeler, H. B. (1986). Humanities in surgery, a life threatening situation: Communicating the diagnosis. *Death Studies* 10, 431–439.
Blatter, J. & Milton, S. (1981). *Art of the holocaust.* New York: Rutland Press.
Bluebond-Langner, M. (1978). *The private worlds of dying children.* Princeton, NJ: Princeton University Press.

Boase, T. S. R. (1972). *Death in the middle ages: Mortality, judgment and remembrance.* New York: McGraw-Hill.

Butler, R. N., & Lewis, M. I. (1977). *Aging and mental health.* St. Louis: The C. V. Mosby Co.

Callahan, D. (1987). *Setting limits.* New York: Simon & Schuster.

Camus, A. (1948). *The plague.* New York: Random House.

Cassell, E. J. (1985). *Talking with patients,* 2 vols. Cambridge, MA: MIT Press.

Cassell, E. J. (1984). *The place of the humanities in medicine.* New York: The Hastings Center.

Choron, J. (1963). *Death and western thought.* New York: Collier Books.

Cohen, K. (1973). *Metamorphosis of a death symbol.* Berkeley, CA: University of California Press.

Coles, R. (1973). *The old ones of New Mexico.* Albuquerque: University of New Mexico Press.

Coles, R. (Ed.). (1984). *William Carlos Williams: The doctor stories.* New York: New Directions.

Coles, R. (1989). *The call of stories. Teaching and the moral imagination.* Boston: Houghton Mifflin.

Cousins, N. (1979). *Anatomy of an illness as perceived by the patient.* New York: Norton.

Cousins, N. (1989). *Head first: the biology of hope.* New York: E. P. Dutton.

Christopher, M. (1977). *The shadow box.* New York: Drama Book Specialists.

Curtin, S. R. (1972). *Nobody ever died of old age: In praise of old people, in outrage at their loneliness.* Boston: Little, Brown and Company.

Cutter, F. (1983). *Art and the wish to die.* Chicago: Nelson-Hall.

Danforth, L. M. (1982). *The death rituals of rural Greece.* Princeton: Princeton University Press.

Dickinson, E. (1951). *The poems of Emily Dickinson,* T. Johnson (Ed.). Cambridge, MA: Belknap Press of Harvard University.

Dillard, A. (1982). *Living by fiction.* New York: Harper & Row.

DuBois, P. M. (1980). *The hospice way of death.* New York: Human Sciences Press.

Eliade, M. (1974). *Death, afterlife, and eschatology: A source book of the history of religions.* New York: Harper & Row.

Farnsworth, E. B. (1988). *Journey through grief.* Atlanta, GA: Susan Hunter Publishing.

Feifel, H. (Ed.). (1965). *The meaning of death.* New York: McGraw-Hill.

Feifel, H. (Ed.). (1977). *New meanings of death.* New York: McGraw-Hill.

Fleshman, B., & Fryrear, J. L. (1981). *The arts in therapy: A comprehensive reference source of the principal art therapies—for core mental health personnel, students and art therapists.* Chicago: Nelson-Hall.

Frankl, V. E. (1959). *Man's search for meaning.* New York: Pocket Books.

Frankl, V. E. (1973). *The doctor & the soul: From psychotherapy to logotherapy.* New York: Random House.

Frazer, J. G. (1977). *The fear of the dead in primitive religion.* New York: Arno Press.

Frost, R. (1958). *The poetry of Robert Frost,* E. Connery Latam (Ed.). New York: Holt, Reinhart and Winston.

Fulton, R. (1976). *Death and identity* (rev. ed.). Bowie, MD: The Charles Press Publishers.

George, D. H., & Nelson, M. A. (1983). *Epitaph and icon: A field guide to the old burying grounds of Cape Cod, Martha's Vineyard, and Nantucket.* New Orleans: Pamassus Imprints.

Gerzon, M. (1982). *A choice of heroes: The changing face of American manhood.* Boston: Houghton Mifflin.

Glaser, B. G., & Strauss, A. (1965). *Awareness of dying.* Chicago: Aldine.

Glaser, B. G., & Strauss, A. (1968). *Time for dying.* Chicago: Aldine.

Goldberg, R., & Tull, R. M. (1983). *The psychosocial dimensions of cancer: A practical guide for health-care providers.* New York: The Free Press.

Gonda, T. A., & Ruark, J. E. (1984). *Dying dignified: The health professional's guide to care.* Menlo Park: Addison-Wesley.

Gorer, G. (1965). *Death, grief and mourning.* New York: Doubleday.

Grof, S., & Halifax, J. (1978). *The human encounter with death.* New York: E. P. Dutton.

Grollman, E. A. (1974). *Concerning death: A practical guide for the living.* Boston: Beacon Press.

Gubrium, J. F. (1976). *Time roles & self in old age.* New York: Human Sciences Press.

Gunther, J. (1965). *Death be not proud.* New York: Harper & Row.

Habaerstein, J., & Lamers, L. (1963). *Funeral customs the world over.* Milwaukee: Bulfin.

Hansen, J. C., & Frantz, T. T. (1984). *Death and grief in the family.* Rockville, MD: Aspen.

Harling, R. (1986). *Steel Magnolias.* New York: Dramatists Play Service.

Hess, B. B. (1980). *Growing old in America.* New Jersey: Transaction.

Hetsler, F. M. (1974). *Death and creativity: An interdisciplinary encounter.* New York: Health Sciences Publishing.

Highwater, J. (1981). *The primal mind: Vision and reality in Indian America.* New York: Harper & Row.

Hilfiker, D. (1985). *Healing the wounds: A physician looks at his work.* New York: Penguin.

Hoffman, W. M. (1985). *As is.* New York: Random House.

Howard, B. (1989). *Epitaphs for the living: Words and images in the time of AIDS.* Dallas: Southern Methodist University Press.

Illich, I. (1976). *Medical nemesis.* New York: Random House.

Irion, P. (1966). *The funeral: Vestige or value?* Nashville: Abingdon Press.

Jampolsky, G. (1979). *Love is letting go of fear.* Millvrae, CA: Celestial Arts.

Janis, E. P., & MacNeil, W. (1977). *Photography within the humanities.* Dambirul, NH: Addison House Publishers.

Joint Commission on Accreditation of Hospitals. (1983). *Hospice standards manual.* Chicago: Author.

Jung, C. (1964). *Man and his symbols.* New York: Dell Publishing.

Jury, M., & Jury, D. (1976). *Gramp.* New York: Grossman Publishers, A Division of Viking Press.

Kalish, R. A. (1977). *Death and dying: Views from many cultures.* Farmingdale, NY: Baywood Publishing Company.

Kart, C. S., Metress, E. S., & Metress, J. F. (1978). *Aging & health: Biological and social perspectives.* Menlo Park: Addison-Wesley Publishing.

Kart, C. S., & Manard, B. B. (1976). *Aging in America: Readings in social gerontology.* Port Washington, NY: Alfred Publishing Company.

Kastenbaum, R., & Aisenberg, R. (1972). *The psychology of death*. New York: Springer Publishing.

Kastenbaum, R. (1977). *Between life & death*. New York: Springer Publishing.

Kastenbaum, R. (1977). *Death, society, & human experience*. St. Louis: The C. V. Mosby Company.

Katz, J. (1984). *The silent world of doctor and patient*. New York: The Free Press.

Kesey, K. (1962). *One flew over the cuckoo's nest*. New York: Viking.

Knobler, N. (1971). *The visual dialogue*. New York: Holt, Rinehart and Winston.

Koch, K. (1978). *I never told anybody: Teaching poetry writing in a nursing home*. New York: Random House.

Konner, M. (1987). *Becoming a doctor: A journey of initiation in medical school*. New York: Viking.

Kopit, A. (1978). *Wings*. New York: Hill & Wang.

Kopp, S. B. (1972). *If you meet the Buddha on the road, kill him!* New York: Bantam Books.

Kubler-Ross, E. (1969). *On death and dying*. New York: Macmillan.

Kubler-Ross, E. (Ed.). (1975). *Death: The final stage of growth*. Englewood Cliffs, NJ: Prentice-Hall.

Kushner, H. (1981). *When bad things happen to good people*. New York: Schocken.

Lamm, M. (1969). *The Jewish way in death and mourning*. New York: Jonathan David Publishers.

Langer, L. L. (1978). *The age of atrocity: Death in modern literature*. Boston: Beacon Press.

Larson, W. W., & Nga, T. T. (1986). *Two women and Vietnam*. New York: Random House.

Lepp, I. (1968). *Death & its mysteries*. Toronto: MacMillan.

Leviton, D. (1991). *Horrendous death, health, and well-being*. Washington, DC: Hemisphere Publishing.

Lewis, C. S. (1961). *A grief revisited*. New York: Seabury Press.

Lifton, R. L. (1974). *Death in life: Survivors of Hiroshima*. New York: Random House.

Lifton, R. L. (1979). *The broken connection*. New York: Simon & Schuster.

Lindemann, E. (1944). Symptamology and management of acute grief. *American Journal of Psychiatry* C1(10), 141–148.

Lynch, J. (1977). *The broken heart*. New York: Basic Books.

Mace, N. L., & Rabbins, P. V. (1981). *The 36-hour day: A family guide to caring for persons with Alzheimer's disease, related dementing illnesses, and memory loss in later life*. Baltimore: The Johns Hopkins University Press.

Maguire, D. (1974). *Death by choice*. New York: Doubleday.

Majno, G. (1975). *The healing hand: Men and wound in the ancient world*. Cambridge, MA: Harvard University Press.

McKee, P., & Kauppinen, H. (1987). *The art of aging: A celebration of old age in western art*. New York: Human Resources Press.

Malmstrom, L., & Kushner, D. (1960). *Four screenplays of Ingmar Bergman: Smiles of a Summer Night, The Seventh Seal, Wild Strawberries, The Magician*. New York: Simon & Schuster.

Marks, S. C., Jr., & Bertman, S. L. (1980). Experiences in learning about death and dying in the undergraduate anatomy curriculum. *Journal of Medical Education* 55, 48–52.

Marris, P. (1974). *Loss and change*. New York: Random House.

McLuhan, M., & Fiore, Q. (1967). *The medium is the message: An inventory of effects*. New York: Bantam Books.

Mitford, J. (1963). *The American way of death*. Greenwich: Crest Book.

Moody, R. (1976). *Life after life*. New York: Bantam.

Parkes, C. M. (1972, but 1986 edition). *Bereavement: Studies of grief in adult life*. Madison, CT: International Universities Press.

Peschel, R. E., & Peschel, E. R. (1986). *When a doctor hates a patient and other chapters in a young physician's life*. Berkeley: University of California Press.

Pike, B. (1988). *Three brass monkeys*. Atlanta, GA: Susan Hunter Publishing.

Pincus, L. (1974). *Death and the family*. New York: Random House.

Pine, V. (1975). *Caretaker of the dead: The American funeral director*. New York: Irvington Publishers.

Ragon, M. (1983). *The space of death: A study of funerary architecture, decoration, and urbanism*. Charlottesville: University Press of Virginia.

Rando, T. (Ed.). (1986). *Loss & anticipatory grief*. Lexington, MA: D. C. Heath.

Rando, T. (1988). *Grieving: How to go on living when someone you love dies*. Lexington, MA: Lexington Books.

Raphael, B. (1983). *The anatomy of bereavement*. New York: Basic Books.

Reiser, D. E., & Rosen, D. H. (1984). *Medicine as a human experience*. Baltimore: University Park Press.

Rossman, P. (1977). *Hospice: Creating new models of care for the terminally ill*. New York: Association Press.

Sacks, O. (1984). *A leg to stand on*. New York: Summit Books.

Sahler, O. (Ed.). (1978). *The child and death*. St. Louis: The C. V. Mosby Company.

Saunders, C. (1984). *The management of terminal malignant disease*. London: Edward Arnold.

Scarry, E. (1985). *The body in pain*. New York: Oxford University Press.

Schneidman, E. (1970). *The deaths of man*. New York: Columbia University Press.

Schneidman, E. (1984). *Death: Current perspectives*. Palo Alto: Mayfield.

Schoenberg, B., Carr, A., Peretz, D., Kutschuv, A. (1970). (Eds.). *Loss and grief*. New York: Columbia University Press.

Schon, D. A. (1970). *The reflective practitioner: How professionals think in action*. New York: Basic Books.

Sexton, A. (1976). *Words for Dr. Y*. Boston: Houghton Mifflin.

Sexton, A. (1976). *The death notebooks*. Boston: Houghton Mifflin.

Shearer, A. (1981). *Disability: Whose handicap?* Oxford: Basil Blackwell Publisher.

Siegel, B. S. (1986). *Love, medicine & miracles: Lessons learned about self-healing from a surgeon's experience with exceptional patients*. New York: Harper & Row.

Silverman, P. R. (1986). *Widow to widow*. New York: Springer.

Simonton, C., & Matthews-Simonton, S. (1978). *Getting well again*. Los Angeles: J. P. Tarcher.

Solzhenitzyn, A. (1969). *Cancer ward*. New York: Straus & Giroux.

Sontag, S. (1978). *Illness as metaphor*. New York: Random House.

Sourkes, B. (1982). *The deepening shade*. Pittsburgh, PA: University of Pittsburgh Press.

Spector, R. E. (1985). *Cultural diversity in health and illness.* East Norwalk, CT: Appleton & Lange.

Stannard, D. E. (1977). *The Puritan way of death: A study in religion, culture, and social change.* New York: Oxford University Press.

Stillion, J. M., McDowell, E. E., & May, J. H. (1989). *Suicide across the life span— Premature exits.* Washington, DC: Hemisphere Publishing.

Stoddard, S. (1978). *The hospice movement: A better way of caring for the dying.* New York: Random House.

Stone, J. (1985). *Renaming the streets.* Baton Rouge: Louisiana State University Press.

Sudnow, D. (1967). *Passing on: The social organization of dying.* Englewood Cliffs: Prentice-Hall.

Thomson, T. L. (1986). *Communication for health professionals.* New York: Harper & Row.

Tolstoy, L. N. (1977). *Master and man and other stories.* Middlesex: Penguin.

Tolstoy, L. N. (1960). *The death of Ivan Ilych.* New York: The New American Library. (Originally published, 1886.)

Trautmann, J. (1981). *Healing arts in dialogue: Medicine and literature.* Edwardsville, IL: Southern Illinois University Press.

Trautmann, J., & Pollard, C. (1982). *Literature and medicine: An annotated bibliography* (rev. ed.). Pittsburgh: University of Pittsburgh Press.

Troup, S., & Greene, W. (1974). *The patient, death and the family.* New York: Charles Scribners Sons.

Ufema, J. (1984). *Brief companions: A composite of true stories about dying persons and the lessons they leave about living.* Fawn Grove: The Mulligan Company.

Veatch, R. M. (1977). *Death, dying and the biological revolution.* New Haven: Yale University Press.

Vermeule, E. (1979). *Aspects of death in early Greek art and poetry.* Berkeley: University of California Press.

Wald, F. (Ed.). (1986). *In quest of the spiritual component of care for the terminally ill.* Collective work, Yale University School of Nursing, New Haven, CT.

Walker, A. (1968). *Once: Poems.* New York: Harcourt Brace Jovanovich.

Weisman, A. (1972). *On dying and denying.* New York: Behavioral.

Wertheimer, M. D., & Bertman, S. L. (1985). Humanities in surgery: Ethics and communication in the surgeon/patient relationship. *Journal of Medical Education* 60.

White, E., & Jones, A. M. (1988). *The darker proof: Stories from a crisis.* New York: New American Library.

Worden, J. W. (1982). *Grief counseling and grief therapy.* New York: Springer Publishing Company.

Appendix 1

Death Attitude Questionnaire

1. How often do you think about your own death?
a. Very frequently (at least once a day).
b. Frequently.
c. Occasionally.
d. Rarely (no more than once a year).
e. Very rarely or never.

2. Has there been a time in your life when you wanted to die?
a. Yes, mainly because of great physical pain.
b. Yes, mainly because of great emotional upset.
c. Yes, mainly to escape an intolerable social or interpersonal situation.
d. Yes, mainly because of great embarassment.
e. Yes, for a reason other than above.
f. No.
g. Other (specify): _____

3. What does death mean to you?
a. The end; the final process of life.
b. The beginning of a life after death; a transition; a new beginning.
c. A joining of the spirit with a universal cosmic consciousness.
d. A kind of endless sleep; rest and peace.
e. Termination of this life but with survival of the spirit.
f. Don't know.
g. Other (specify): _____

4. What aspects of your own death are the most distasteful to you?
a. I could no longer have any experiences.
b. I am afraid of what might happen to me if there is a life after death.
c. I am uncertain as to what might happen to my body after death.
d. I could no longer provide for my dependents.
e. It would cause grief to my relatives and friends.
f. All of my plans and projects would come to an end.
g. The process of dying might be painful.
h. Other (specify): _____

5. How do you feel about having an autopsy done on your body?
a. Approve.
b. Don't care one way or another.
c. Disapprove.
d. Strongly disapprove.

6. If it were entirely up to you, how would you like to have your body disposed of after you have died?
a. Burial.
b. Cremation.
c. Donation to medical school or science.
d. I am indifferent.

209

7. **Would you be willing to donate your heart for transplantation after you die?**
a. Yes, to anyone.
b. Yes, but only to a relative or a friend.
c. I have a strong feeling against it.
d. No.

8. **What kind of funeral would you prefer?**
a. Normal, as large as possible.
b. Small, relatives and close friends only.
c. Whatever my survivors want.
d. None.
e. Other (specify): _____

9. **How do you feel about "lying in state" in an open casket at your funeral?**
a. Approve.
b. Don't care one way or the other.
c. Disapprove.
d. Strongly disapprove.
e. Other (specify): _____

Adapted from a questionnaire on you and death devised by Schneidman, E. (1970) *Psychology Today* 4, 67–72.

Appendix 2

Facing Death: A Most Memorable Image

Name (optional) _____ Occupation _____ Age ___ Sex ___

(a) Please select one image from the presentation. The image might have been disturbing, consoling, provocative, amusing, whatever. Identify or describe the image briefly, and in the space below, please give the reason for your choice.

(b) Please comment on the meaning the image has for you at this point in time, personally or professionally.

(c) Additional thoughts or comments on the presentation as a whole (what you liked best, least . . . attitude changes . . .) would also be appreciated.

(d) Would you like the bibliography of resources when it is compiled and/ or a copy of a specific image? (please specify)

yes _____ no _____

Name _____ Phone number _____

Address _____

Appendix 3
First-Year Course Syllabus (Fall Semester)

Medical Humanities: On Dissection, Dying and Death
Instructors: Sandra L. Bertman, Ph.D.
and Sandy C. Marks, Jr., Ph.D.

It is our responsibility to remember that medicine is not only a science, but also the art of letting our own individuality interact with the individuality of the patient.

Albert Schweitzer

The first patient to whom you are introduced is a dead one. Dissection of the human body often raises questions about the source of cadavers, bodily trespass, invasion of privacy, life, and death. We encourage you to explore attitudes toward dissection and death as you experience the first year of medical school in the belief that facing and expressing the aversions, fears, and fantasies associated with human dissection can help prepare you not only for academic work in the anatomy laboratory but also for the emotional work that patient care—the "laying on of hands"— implies. Our aim is to lay the foundation for future professional development in the context of the physician-patient relationship and for continuing personal self-inquiry and exploration of humanistic, ethical, and existential issues in medicine.

The first-year course consists of the following experiences.

1. Anticipating dissection: Assignment to reflect on and create an image pertaining to dissection just prior to entering medical school.
2. Facing dissection: Course overview: Introduction to themes and timeline of the course, the history of dissection, the anatomical gift, and the parallels between dissection and patient care.
3. Meeting the cadavers: Tour of dissection laboratory in small groups w/cell biology faculty and second-year students.
4. Facing dissection: Coping styles: Exploration of the experience of dissection through analysis of students' own images. Lecture pre-

sentation followed by small group discussions with cell biology and clinical faculty.

5. "The Anatomy Lesson": Film and discussion of a balletic interpretation of Rembrandt's masterpiece and traditional and contemporary responses to dissection as portrayed in fiction and the arts.

6. Facing death: Coping styles and questions of values: Amphitheatre presentation of the experience of dying from diagnosis through death depicted in the visual arts, fiction, and popular culture followed by small group discussions.

7. Memorial service: Student-designed service of commemoration.

Readings: Packets of related fiction, poetry, and essays will be distributed and are on reserve in the library; Packet: Bertman, S., "Facing Dissection . . . ." Selections include poetry and prose by John Stone, E. E. Cummings, Igor Webb, W. C. Williams, S. Plath, medical students, and other physician writers, including the following selections:

Platt, M. (1975). Looking at the body. In *Hastings center reports, 5*. Feelings aroused by being alone with a dead body, various kinds of looking (including overlooking), and professional similarities between anatomist and painter are articulately discussed.

Sharkey, F. (1982). Ingmar Wollenstrum. In *A parting gift*, chapter 2. New York: St. Martin's Press. Pediatrician traces to her dissection experiences the development of emotional detachment as her sole coping mechanism for facing the death of patients. Entire book is worthwhile.

Stone, I. (1961). The flight. In *The agony and the ecstasy*, chapter 4. New York: Doubleday. Michelangelo's "sacriligious errand," performing human dissections to gain the precious knowledge he needs as an apprentice sculptor, raises concerns similar to those voiced by medical students. Emotions of terror, revulsion, pity, contamination, and personal vulnerability are worked through and ultimately replaced by fascination, excitement, and joy as he loses himself in the details of the experience.